THE ACCIDENTAL PILGRIM

Travels with a Celtic Saint

DAVID MOORE

The Accidental Pilgrim

Travels with a Celtic Saint

Hodder Headline Ireland

First published in 2004 by Hodder Headline Ireland
This edition published in 2005

A Hodder Headline Ireland paperback

1 3 5 4 2

A CIP catalogue record for this title is available from the British Library

ISBN 0 340 83248 7

Typeset in Plantin Light by Hodder Headline Ireland

Printed and bound by
Clays Ltd, St Ives plc

Hodder Headline Ireland
8 Castlecourt Centre
Castleknock
Dublin 15
Ireland
A division of Hodder Headline
338 Euston Road
London NW1 3BH

Visit the author's website on www.accidentalpilgrim.com

David Moore was raised in England and spent many childhood summers in Ireland. A graduate of Cambridge and Trinity College Dublin, his freelance journalism has appeared in the *Irish Times*, the *Irish Examiner* and the *Illustrated London News*. After a stint in the Internet industry in Kansas, followed by a move to San Fransisco in the middle of the dot-com frenzy, he returned to Ireland. He is recently married, and lives in Dublin.

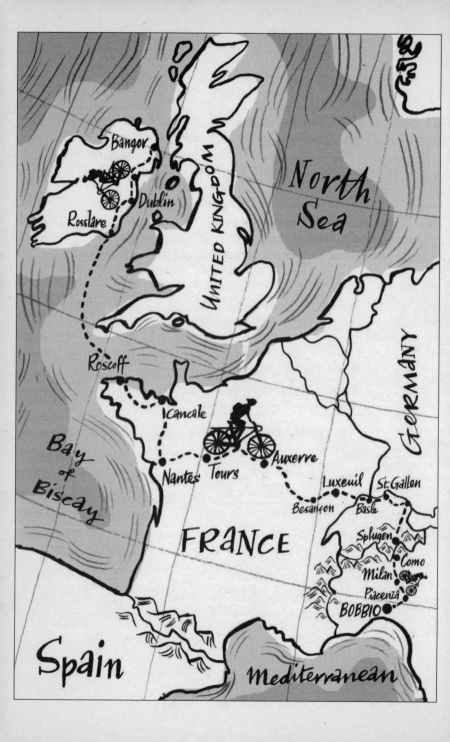

Contents

To my nephew Abhisheka Columbanus
and his big brother Tejomaya

1

Over the Top

So I'm sitting in a tiny café in a place called Splugen. It's a Saturday towards the end of September, and the weather is cloudy, with mist draped over the views outside. I'm finishing off my lunchtime soup (not sure exactly what's in it – my German is terrible). I'm shaking a little and feel light-headed, and I'm watching the other diners with fevered intensity.

A young Italian couple are relaxing over their beer, keeping an indulgent eye on their daughter, who's fascinated by the old jukebox in the corner. A well-turned-out Swiss couple are sitting in the corner with their dog curled up obediently at their feet. The proprietor and his wife are at another table about to start their own late lunch.

It's been well over a month since I left Dublin, and I've travelled more than two thousand kilometres clear across France and Switzerland. But today's the day I pedal my bike over the Alps.

My pasta arrives and I launch into it, hoping the starch will keep me grounded and give me the fuel I need. I've already ridden for twenty-six kilometres uphill today, but there's another nine kilometres of steep climbing to get to the top of the Splugen Pass, before the long descent on the

Italian side of the border. Laden with panniers, the bike handles like an oil tanker, and stopping is gradual at best. In the battle between gravity and cantilever brakes, gravity would win, especially in the rain. So there's nothing for it. I just have to get on the bike and combine two days' riding into one while it's still dry.

After the food and some coffee I feel better, but I remount and head out of town with a knot of tension at the base of my spine. There's snow on the tops of the mountains, which is where I'm going. Poring over maps at home, I'd never even considered that there'd still be snow up here at this time of year. A sign tells me the pass is open except to large vehicles, and then the hairpins begin. Eight or ten loops up the hillside in bottom gear and I'm looking down over the town nestling in its high valley. Then, round the corner, the road straightens. My legs are burning and my heart's racing, but I can just about keep going like this for now. A few cars pass me, and I look for some reaction from them, but the sensible Swiss-registered Audi estates slide by mutely until a young Italian in his sporty two-seater Mercedes comes towards me and honks his horn, waving. Dude.

The road is heading up into a snowy bowl, with no obvious exit. The altimeter on my watch shows me gaining elevation in five-metre blocks – 1845, 1850. It's colder now, and my top is zipped to the neck despite all the heat my effort's generating. Ahead is another set of hairpins as the road zigzags up into the mist.

I can't believe I'm doing this. A surge of excitement jolts me. My legs are feeling surprisingly good now, and a rhythm comes easily as I'm out of the saddle round the bends, and sitting down again for the straights. I'm at 1900 metres now, and the top of the pass is at 2115. The highest mountain in Ireland is half that height. There's snow on the side of the road, and I stop on the outside of a bend and reach down to run my fingers through it.

The mist is closing in, but it doesn't matter that I can't see the higher peaks around me. I'm just looking for the next corner, as each one comes to represent a day of all the riding it took to get here. This one is the day I rode to Château-giron, this one is the slog into Besançon. This one is that morning coming out of Avallon, and this one the off-road excursion on the way to Baden. I grab a quick look around and out loud say 'Thank you' to the mountains, to the days I've put in to get myself here, to the bike (especially to the bike). I'm going to make it to the top.

After the next fold in the ribbon of road, I head round a corner to a building, the first since Splugen. It's a restaurant, but up still further is another structure. With melted snow running down the road and visibility down to ten metres, I pass the customs post. Inside three guys in uniform are watching television. They glance out of the window at this Englishman who's ridden up the mountain on a bike, and wave me through without bothering to come out and get cold. I'm in Italy.

It's a shame I can't see any of it. I stop for a self-timed photo in front of a sign with an Italian flag on it, and put on my jacket for the descent. As mountain climbers will tell you, getting to the top seems like the big achievement, but getting down is often the hardest part. The first few kilometres are not so bad; past a lake of smooth silver water, with a father and son fishing in silhouette on the shore, and down through a tiny collection of houses.

But then ahead of me looms a narrow tunnel. I have a faint recollection of seeing some pictures on the Internet of the Italian side of the Splugen Pass, with tunnels and galleries stacked above each other in the cliff face, joined by hairpin bends so that the road you were just driving over becomes the roof of the next loop. But there's no time to recall much detail before I'm launched into darkness. My bike lights are useless – I can't see the road ahead. Or the walls. Or the ceiling. Or my hands on the handlebars. I've got a vague sense of being in the middle of the road, and I know I'm still going downhill pretty fast, but I'm blind. I hit a pothole and the bike bucks me. The tyres swish through some water that's dripped from the roof. I'm half standing over the saddle with the pedals level, trying to stay light on the bike, to let it ride itself, because that's all I can do. Then there's a smudge of white in the distance off to the left a little and it widens quickly: the light at the end of the tunnel. I'm living a cliché.

I'm through it and back out into the world. Holy living fuck. I brake and lean into a hairpin and see another tunnel ahead. This time two cars are coming in the opposite direction, their lights illuminating the narrow road and the cratered wet surface. I can see more but the roaring engines fill my ears, the noise echoing round the enclosed space. With the sound bouncing about it's impossible to tell if there are any vehicles behind me. I hold on and fight the disorientation. Next comes a gallery with a couple of openings in the side wall, for illumination, but it drops more steeply than the previous two, and there's a sign announcing eight more hairpins ahead.

I concentrate intently round the steep bends – those to the left are easier, as you're on the outside and the camber allows you to feed the bike into them while still moving quickly. Right-hand ones are much harder, as you scrub off speed coming into them, and turn sharply as the road drops away on the inside of the bend. Run wide and you're into cars being gunned into the corners on the way up. At the back of my mind a voice is saying, 'This is very dangerous. I'm not happy. I shouldn't be here,' but there's no choice. I take a deep breath and try to focus on the next tunnel. There's no light in this one either and I have a vision of me slapping the bike down on the Tarmac as a car comes round the corner. I can't tell where I am on the road, but at least I'm going fast enough that I'm not in there too long.

Then the kinks unwind for a time and I shoot through the first real settlement on the way down, with the road still dropping insanely. The speed on the trip computer keeps rising: 45 k.p.h., 50, 55. And cars are still streaking past me on the narrow road. More hairpins, and my body is tight from being in the same stretched position for so long, but the air is warmer and the mist has cleared, revealing wooded slopes and narrow gorges.

And suddenly I'm coming to a halt at a crossroads in terracotta Chiavenna. There are crowds wandering around, little mopeds zipping between the cars, and there's the chatter of Saturday-afternoon shopping. I'm quivering, my head's buzzing, and I feel emptied – I've left it all on the mountain. I shake my head and swear quietly to myself. The scene is so ordinary and so far removed from my last few hours I might as well have been teleported into this town. I've ridden my bike nearly a mile into the sky from where I started this morning, then descended madly for thirty kilometres in what felt like ten minutes.

But the man I had followed from Ireland had made the same journey in his sixties wearing sandals, so I wasn't so hot.

2

Paul Weller, Lady Gregory and James Bond

I blame Paul Weller for everything. I was sitting in the Olympia Theatre in Dublin waiting for him to take the stage, talking to my housemate Garrett about what I'd do if I owned a car. 'I wouldn't use it around town, but I'd head off down the country. Or I'd go over to England and visit all those cathedral cities I've never been to – Durham, Lichfield, Wells, Winchester.'

'Sounds good.' Garrett was more interested in when Paul Weller would appear.

'And Lindisfarne. Always wanted to go there.'

And this was when it happened. Thinking about one monastery led to thoughts of others, a door in the recesses of my mind opened, and out came a half-remembered itinerary I'd learned about in college. 'Or I'd take the ferry to Brittany, and follow St Columbanus across France and over the Alps to Italy.' If I'd stopped there, it might not have been too bad. But I had to go on: 'Of course, if I was really going to do it, I'd have to go on a bike.'

I was doomed. Dublin is a city full of ideas – the pubs and cafés resound with people plotting the next big thing in film, or literature, or (until recently) technology. Everybody's doing one thing when they'd rather be doing something else.

Maybe pints of Guinness work as radio receivers for stray notions that are floating around looking for a chance to happen. Of course, many of these ideas aren't very good, and many more are good but come to the wrong person. But sometimes the right ideas come to the right people, and that's when the trouble really starts. That was what happened to me.

There seemed to be three conditions necessary in the recruitment of someone to retrace the route of an obscure seventh-century monk across Europe: the first was an interest in the period of history. It's not called the Dark Ages for nothing and, distracted by the promise of lots of historical sources, some vibrant characters and a hankering after relevance to the present day, most historians tend to skip the unfashionable block of centuries from AD500 to 1000.

But not me. A bookish boy, I'd been fond of Tolkien and Dungeons and Dragons. *Robin of Sherwood* had been my favourite television programme. As I got older, my fascination with swords and myths turned into a slightly more respectable interest in early medieval history. One day in the sixth form I'd flicked through a university prospectus and stumbled across 'Anglo-Saxon, Norse and Celtic'. It was the first course description in an alphabetical list, and I was instantly sold on illuminated manuscripts, Pictish symbol stones and obscure Insular Latin writers such as Aldhelm and Byrtferth of Ramsey. I scoffed at the Renaissance as an event so recent it was impossible to assess its true importance. (I've often wondered whether, if the course had been called 'Norse, Celtic and Anglo-Saxon', I would now be an anthropologist or an archaeologist.) I hadn't opened any of the books since I'd left college, but at least I had a vague notion of who St Columbanus was.

The second condition was an interest in cycling. While at university in Cambridge, I'd walked rather than cycled, but Dublin is bigger so I'd started riding around town and watching the Tour de France on television. Soon I was doing sponsored rides to Kilkenny and carrying my expensive bike up the stairs at work to sit beside me all day. Things had got out of hand when I'd worked in America for three years, and mountain-biked in Colorado and Wyoming and had a regular ride that took me through downtown San Francisco and over the Golden Gate Bridge. Now I was back in rainy Dublin I thought things might calm down, but I fell in with a couple of cycling friends and neighbours and there was no hope for me. (I'd tell you how many bikes the three of us have between us in our little corner of the street but unless you were a bicycle thief you'd laugh.) But for all my cycling, I couldn't repair them, and I'd never stuck all my kit on the back of the bike and headed off on a long tour.

Third, you'd need to have the time to do it. After eighteen months in Kansas and eighteen more in San Francisco, I'd returned to Dublin. I'd worked for Internet companies and, with dumb luck that I now pass off as remarkable prescience, I'd decided right before the high-tech economy tanked that the time was right to do something else. I didn't think it would be riding a bike to Italy, but by the time Paul Weller had finished his encore with 'That's Entertainment', my mind was racing. I appeared to be the perfect candidate to carry out this idea – and I had no good reason not to do it. Well, there were thousands of reasons, but I would do some research – I might not end up going.

Readjusting to life in Dublin had been harder than I'd anticipated. I found the city dirty and unfriendly, and too focused around pub culture. I'd come back because I had a house here, but I felt in some ways as if I'd outgrown Dublin. I wasn't taking advantage of all it had to offer in terms of nightlife and culture, but I still had to put up with all the hassles of living in a large and increasingly expensive city. I had a notion to move, but no real incentive to go anywhere. After years in cubicle hell, doing things I didn't care about, I had also vowed that I'd never work in an office again, but had no real picture of what I should do instead. My challenge was to think of something before my savings ran out.

I'd been home for four months, and had drifted through the weeks doing almost nothing. This may sound ideal, but it soon emerged that I suffered from both an Anglo-Saxon work ethic (from my English upbringing) and a Catholic guilt complex (thanks to my Irish mother). Pure-bred English people work hard and play hard – my inner English lad said, 'You should be largin' it, mate. You worked hard in San Francisco, and now you can go mental. Top banana.' But as soon as I tried it, the Catholic guilt complex kicked in. 'Would you look at himself there, living the life of Riley. It's well for some. Who does he think he is at all? He should go and find some more work to do.' So I did.

The first thing was to find out more about St Columbanus. I returned to my old haunts in Trinity College and the National Library in Dublin, and quickly established the basic facts: Columbanus was born around AD550 and was one of the first of the early medieval Irish monks who set off across Europe, founding monasteries as they went. He trained in Comgall's monastery in Bangor, County Down, but eventually felt a calling to become an 'exile for Christ', and sailed for France with twelve followers. He crossed France, and settled in Luxeuil in the Haut-Saône region, where he founded three monasteries. After twenty years there he was expelled from the country for annoying the royal family – even the Pope found him difficult to deal with – and headed into the Alps to found a monastery at Bregenz on the shore of Lake Constance. Around a year later, he continued over the mountains into northern Italy, ending up in a small town called Bobbio in the Apennines near Piacenza. He died in 615, and within a century around a hundred more monasteries had been founded by his pupils and followers. His foundations became beacons of scholarship and teaching in a Europe that had suffered waves of barbarian attacks and related chaos.

The distances involved and the influence this one Irishman had were remarkable enough, but even more so is that a wide selection of Columbanus's writings still survives – letters, sermons, the Rules he wrote for his French monasteries, even some poetry. This collection of work represents the earliest writings by an Irish person that we have, making Columbanus the first Irish man of letters.

As well as Columbanus's own writings, one of his Italian followers, named Jonas, wrote a history of his master's life within thirty years of the saint's death. Jonas's dour translator maintains the life is 'written in a barbarous Latinity', but it contains a remarkable amount of detail about Columbanus, gathered from people who were there at the time.

All this was very promising. Not only would it be possible

to work out his route, but it might also be possible to build up something of a picture of the man himself, despite the fourteen centuries between us. I was enjoying being back in the libraries again. My sister argues that it takes at least five years to recover from being at university, but I maintain that there's no getting over it. When I hear guests on *Desert Island Discs* prefacing one of their selections with 'Oh, this reminds me of my time at college. Best years of my life,' I choke on my cornflakes. To appear on the programme you have to be a success in your chosen field, yet forty years on, people are looking back on their whole adult lives as something of a let-down after their thirty-six months of freewheeling adolescent excess. I'd not been very excessive myself during college, so I welcomed the chance to try to be a better (that is, worse) student. I got up late, put in a few hours with the books, then sloped off for mid-afternoon coffees that drifted into early-evening drinks. After the grind of work, this was great. My commute was a stroll into town. My email stopped being full of production schedules, CVs of prospective employees and the agenda for the weekly team meeting; instead it was corny jokes and lunch arrangements with fellow slackers.

Then the challenge of the Manuscripts Room arrived to impose some structure on my life. I'd come across references to two books written in the 1890s by a woman called Margaret Stokes, a member of a storied Dublin Anglo-Irish family. Her grandfather, Whitley Stokes, had fought with the United Irishmen alongside Wolfe Tone (who described him as 'the very best man I have ever known'). Her father, Dr William Stokes, had been a physician to Queen Victoria and president of the Royal Irish Academy, while her brother, also called Whitley, had spent twenty years in India as a civil servant but was best known for his translations of Old Irish texts. Margaret was an artist and illustrator, deeply involved in the Celtic Revival movement, and she had travelled to France and Italy to trace the paths of several of the Irish monks on the Continent.

This was perfect for me, but first I had to get to the books, which appeared to be kept at the centre of a labyrinth. Garrett, a Ph.D. student at Trinity and an old hand at this, briefed me on the strategy for gaining access to the Manuscripts Room.

'First you go into the shop downstairs in the old library, where the tourists come in to see the Book of Kells.'

'Check.'

'Then go up the stairs past the no-entry sign, into the Long Room.'

'Is that allowed?'

'Of course. Then it's past the guard at the top of the stairs, and under the rope. Along to the end of the room, and you'll see a set of double doors.'

'Is there a sign or anything on the door?'

'Yeah, I think it says, "Private, Keep Out".'

'I see.'

'Now, when you open the door an alarm might go off, but don't worry about that. Go down a flight of marble stairs, past a huge painting of the Battle of the Boyne.'

'Down? But didn't you say the Manuscripts Room is above the Long Room?'

'It is. Turn right, and in the corner is a small lift. Go into the lift. I don't think it says so, but you want the third floor. You'll come out at the reception desk for the room. Then you're on your own.'

Librarians make it clear that their sense of duty is to the books, not the people who want to read them, and the most rigorous librarians of all oversee the rare books or manuscript rooms, guarding their priceless holdings like a dragon on a hoard of gold. So when I appeared before the surprisingly glamorous female librarian at the desk with my request, she seemed disappointed. Another person come to disturb us. Why can't they just leave us alone with the collection? I was all but frisked for pens before being allowed in with my pencil and notepad, and seated at a set of tables in the middle of the room with a grey foam stand in front of me. While the books were being retrieved I tried to work out why Margaret Stokes's works were in the Manuscripts Room – they were published books from a little over a hundred years ago, only yesterday by the standards of a library like Trinity's. The two green hardbacks were brought by a younger librarian, who placed the first one on the foam stand, and instructed me on the use of the lengths of card and leaded ribbons to turn the pages and hold the book open. She then retreated to her desk in the corner, from where she could survey the room.

The book on the stand was *Six Months in the Apennines, or a Pilgrimage in Search of Vestiges of the Irish Saints in Italy*, published in 1892. I opened it, and saw the reason for all the care over this modest tome – inside the front cover was the *Ex Libris* stamp of Lady Gregory, stalwart of the Celtic Revival, friend to W.B. Yeats and co-founder of the Abbey Theatre. I had an image of her sitting in the garden at Coole Park, and turning to Yeats. 'Willie, have you read this new book by Margaret? It's quite delightful.'

'Not now, Augusta, I'm trying to write. Can you think of a word that rhymes with "Innisfree"?'

While I was reading about plucky Margaret arriving in Italian towns and commanding a passing boy to carry her camera up the side of a hill for her, the phone rang for the librarian and she dealt with a query from an American genealogist. She explained patronisingly that just because someone had been admitted to the college didn't mean they had gained a degree, so they might well not show up in some of the records. While spelling out her email address, she seemed to lose patience. 'No, that's T, C, D. No, D. Yes, Trinity College, Dublin . . . So, TCD dot IE . . . Dot. IE. I for "indigenous", E for "Erin".' Indigenous Erin? Librarians.

Most of my time in the libraries was spent establishing a route to follow. Born somewhere in Leinster (possibly around Carlow), Columbanus had lived in the monastery in Bangor, County Down, near Belfast, until he was in his forties. So I was definitely going up to Northern Ireland before anything else. In 590 he had set sail for France. Now Bangor doesn't offer ferry crossings to anywhere, so I'd have to travel down to Rosslare in the south-east to start my own voyage. Some scholars think he landed in Cornwall (there are two places that appear to bear his name there), but most agree that he headed straight for Brittany, which was easier for me. So that was the first part of the journey taken care of – up and down the east coast of Ireland, then on to a ferry.

Columbanus spent some time in Brittany before visiting one of the Frankish kings, who granted him land for a monastery near Luxeuil in eastern France. The route he took to get there, or even where he met the king, is unknown, but he probably went along the Loire, then struck out eastwards through Chalon-sur-Saône and Besançon.

We have more detail about his return journey to the coast of France. After nearly twenty years around Luxeuil he fell out of favour with the royal family, and was escorted off the premises. Columbanus's hagiographer, Jonas, lists the towns the party of Irishmen went through as they headed for the port at Nantes. Again, they headed cross-country to the Loire, and this time took a boat down the river. Columbanus was supposed to sail back to Ireland, but Jonas tells of a miracle that stopped his boat sailing out of the port, and it certainly seems his guards lost interest after escorting him thus far. Instead of heading home, the party of monks headed back inland, but further north.

Political history at this time in France is a hugely confusing succession of Sigeberts and Sigismunds, Theudeberts and Theuderics, all fighting for control of different parts of the country, which was loosely divided into three kingdoms. Columbanus's dispute was with the king of Burgundy, a Theuderic, but he was welcomed by the king's relatives, who controlled the other two realms.

After travelling through Paris and Metz, Columbanus reached the Rhine, and headed up the river, aiming for Bregenz on Lake Constance, where he had been granted permission to found another monastery. After a year, the changing political situation (the term medieval historians use to describe brutal battles and internecine strife) forced him to move again, and this time he went southwards to Italy, where the Lombards had recently seized power. He was welcomed at court in Milan, and granted land in Bobbio, forty kilometres south-west of Piacenza. He had been in Bobbio only a year when he died in November 615.

Columbanus's zigzag peregrinations were much more

extensive than I'd imagined. It would have been impressive enough if he had travelled the shortest route from Bangor to Bobbio, but he had also crossed France three times, and navigated a sizeable chunk of what's now Switzerland. To follow every last yard of the route would involve a lot of repetition, and would also see me travelling huge distances to visit towns in which at most Columbanus might possibly have spent a night. Some places were clearly more important than others, and while a range of detours was easy to plan on a map, I was going to have to travel every last yard under my own steam. So a compromise plan emerged. From Brittany I'd head to Luxeuil along the Loire (we can definitely place Columbanus in Nantes, Tours and Orléans), then press on to Switzerland meeting the Rhine at Basle, cutting out the German loop. Then through Switzerland to Bregenz, which turns out to be in Austria (who knew?), before turning south over the Alps, down to Lake Como and the last leg through Milan to Bobbio. I sat in the elegant expanse of the National Library reading room with *The Times Atlas*, checking off distances on the edge of a piece of paper. The marks went along one side of the sheet, round the corner and back down the other side: 2500 kilometres, give or take quite a lot. Over 1500 miles.

It seemed a very long way on a bike, but there were two obvious attractions to the route. First, it went through lovely places – Brittany, along the Loire, Lakes Constance and Como, the Lombard Plain – if Columbanus had founded monasteries in Belgium, I'm not sure I would have followed him. Also, after three years on another continent it would be good to reconnect with my European cousins, especially by following an Irishman who was so well accepted all the way from Ulster to Lombardy.

The second source of appeal was that if I was riding to Italy, I'd need some new kit. The gearhead in me rejoiced. The bike itself was already taken care of – putting aside the tricksy bikes I'd been riding in the States, all ceramic particulate frames and NASA-derived drivetrains, I dug around in the cupboard under the stairs and pulled out an old Dawes touring bike, made from unfashionable steel. I'd bought it years ago almost by accident, and found it slow and dull, and never given it a fair chance. It was, however, the perfect choice for a long trip: comfortable to ride, with a rack on the back for attaching panniers, and a set of low gears that meant you could spin along in very pedestrian fashion. It was also a simple machine, with gear shifters on the down tube of the frame and old-style cantilever brakes. I'm mechanically illiterate, so I didn't want to be fussing with rear shocks or funky handlebar shifters on the side of a rainy road in the middle of nowhere.

There were lots of other things I did need to get, though, and over the next weeks I immersed myself in the arcane world of the serious bike tourist. I scoured the Internet for gear reviews and bargain prices, assembling a shopping list to make James Bond envious. The great outdoors had come a long way since my camping début on the primary-school summer trip to Dorset. Everything was now technical, breathable and wickable, and made from Gore-Tex, Taslan, Rip-Stop, mesh, fleece or Cordura. If it didn't fold up to the size of a cigarette packet and boast so many features that you couldn't write them all on the tiny box, then it wasn't worth having. Being at one with nature had been replaced by ignoring it entirely inside your bubble of performance products.

But I guessed I would need all the help I could get, so when the freakishly light but devilishly expensive packages started arriving, I felt heartened that there were few scrapes my combined altimeter, barometer, temperature gauge, compass, heart-rate monitor and watch could not get me out of. Of course, Columbanus had had much more modest equipment, and I would perhaps have done well to recall his wise comment that 'The man to whom little is not enough will not benefit from more.' But it was clear that while I might be following his route, I would be spending my days in more comfort than he had. I planned to camp some of the time, but to stay in hotels in the larger towns, and eat a great deal of good food. This set me at odds with Columbanus's instructions to his monks: 'Let the monks' food be poor and taken in the evening, such to avoid repletion.' But after my years in America, eating my way elegantly across Europe sounded great. But first I had an appointment in a place known to the locals as Norn Iron.

3

Mounds and Monasteries

When Columbanus left his home in Leinster to travel up to the north of Ireland, his mother threw herself to the floor in the doorway and begged him to stay. Showing a single-mindedness that would mark his future dealings with the world, the young saint-to-be stepped over her and headed out of the door. He'd never see her again.

Over fourteen hundred years later, when I left my home in Leinster to follow in his footsteps, my bike threw itself to the floor in the doorway. It was the first time it had been loaded with all the gear I'd bought and it didn't want me to go. I struggled manfully to get it out the door. 'You're coming with me whether you like it or not,' I said to it, leaning it upright outside the front door.

The four-day trip I planned was practice with the bike, and a chance to put myself in places that Columbanus had seen. The research and planning had been entertaining but I had to find out if I could do this touring thing. And if I enjoyed it.

Once on the move, the machine proved easier to handle than I'd expected, and with the June sun shining weakly I headed slowly out of Dublin, aiming for Newgrange, a somewhat anachronistic place for me to start my explorations.

The Boyne valley near Drogheda is blessed with a great

range of archaeological and historical sites, with Newgrange premier among them. It's a huge mound containing a passage grave, built before the first stepped pyramid in Egypt, and a thousand years before Stonehenge. At dawn on the winter solstice, the rising sun shines up the passage in the tomb and into the main chamber (although as this is Ireland, it's as likely that it's cloudy, and everyone goes home and waits for next year).

Columbanus would have passed this way en route to Bangor, but in 570 the tomb was overgrown and would have been little more than a weirdly shaped hill. But I was passing, so I called in. At the interpretive centre, you book your place on one of the coaches heading to Newgrange, or the other nearby mound of Knowth, and are rewarded with a sticker announcing the time the coach leaves. I was met by a very smiley young receptionist who stuck my two stickers on my cycling jersey. I felt about ten years old. 'You should really stick them on upside down, so I can read them when I look down,' I said.

'Right you are!' She took them off and stuck them on again the other way up. This was great: I was getting a few of the hundred thousand welcomes normally reserved for visitors to the country.

Our guide met us at the entrance to Newgrange. Greg was wearing three fleece tops, and his young face was a weathered red that told of the alternate damage of sun- and windburn. He looked like he'd been up and down Everest rather than standing around a field in County Meath all summer, but he was better dressed for the increasingly windy and overcast day than most of his charges, who were determinedly still wearing their summer holiday clothes.

With his back against one of the standing stones near the entrance to the passage, he ran through the basic facts of the tomb's construction, carefully stressing that these were just the latest interpretations, and they might all be proved wrong in the future. So that's why they call it an interpretive centre. As well as the sun alignment at the winter solstice, there are suggestions that the site may also be aligned to the moon and to Jupiter, although Greg was particularly circumspect about this.

We were led carefully up the passage and into the central chamber. When you're piled into it with fifteen sundry Germans, Americans and Swiss, bright lighting and the rustle of waterproofs, it's hard to get a sense of its majesty. And while you can acknowledge its age, appreciating what that means is near impossible. Your brain just files it away as 'really, really old'. But staring up at the vaulted ceiling, I certainly felt removed from my own time. Greg told us of recent trance experiments by a team from the University of Michigan in which participants felt they were being drawn up into the spiral vaulting of the roof. Here his mask of academic neutrality slipped a little: 'That's what they say, anyway. But they were off their heads, so . . .'

In fact, Greg wasn't averse to trying to put us into an altered state. He switched off the main lights, and wove a moody prose poem describing the light of the summer solstice creeping up to the level of the roof box at the entrance, and edging along the narrow passage before illuminating the whole of the central chamber. God knows how many times he had done this same thing, but his enthusiasm for the place and his job shone through, especially when he pointed out there were two main ways to see the solstice there for real (weather permitting): become president of your country, or a guide at Newgrange. He'd obviously gone for plan B, and fair play to him.

The minibuses to and from the interpretive centre allow the numbers visiting the sites to be carefully controlled, but it does make for a rather disjointed experience, as you return to the centre to await the next bus to your second destination. I was heading for Knowth, a lesser known but in many ways more impressive Neolithic tomb. Just five of us were on the bus for the last tour of the day, and we were met at the gate by our new guide, Sharon, hidden somewhere inside a big Lowe Alpine waterproof with the hood up. The major difference between Knowth and Newgrange is that the site at Knowth was in almost continuous use from around BC3000 to the Anglo-Norman invasion, when a house was built on top of the largest mound. Around the main mound there are several smaller burial mounds each as high as a house, as well as souterrains, and other graves from a range of periods. There are signs of late Iron Age and early Christian use, so the place was inhabited during Columbanus's time.

Because of the later structures built above them, the two passages into the main mound have collapsed so access is only possible if you crawl in on your hands and knees, and Sharon wouldn't let us do that. But with the layers of history heaped on top of each other and a little more room to think, I preferred the site to Newgrange.

I retrieved my bike from the visitor centre, and set off for the bed and breakfast I'd booked nearby. If I'd been riding my skinny road bike, the seventy-odd kilometres I'd come would have been an easy morning's work, to be rounded off with a coffee at an Italian café on the way home, like I was a

European pro rider out on a training spin. But my slow plodder of a touring bike required a different attitude to achievement. It was a success to have covered the distance at all and still be able to walk when I got off the bike.

My evening meal in Drogheda was less successful. Rain began to fall as I rode the short distance into town, the restaurants recommended at the B&B were closed, and I'd forgotten the map that showed all the others. The only place I could find was called The Lanterns. Half of it was devoted to a takeaway, the other half had seating past a machine full of cuddly toys that you could try to hook with a remote-control claw on a cable – always a sign of culinary excellence. It was quiet, and the radio was playing country music. I've never understood the enthusiasm for bad country music in large parts of Ireland, and I sat through 'What Part of "No" Don't You Understand?' while downing my fish and chips. Not an auspicious start to months of eating alone. I'd enjoyed the day, but I was going to be with myself all the time, trying to find restaurants, hotels and campsites in towns I'd never been in before. Every night. Suddenly it seemed a long way to Italy.

It's tempting to think that Columbanus's life in the monastery at Bangor was all silence and quiet reflection. In fact, early Christian monasteries in Ireland were carefully placed near major communication routes. As Jonas remarks, Columbanus was 'born amid the beginnings of his race's faith', and in the sixth and seventh centuries Christianity was taking hold in Ireland from the top down. Many monasteries were founded by local royal families, with the abbacy often passed down within the founding family. Columba (also known as

Columcille), who founded the influential monastery of Iona, was of the Uí Niall line in Donegal, and St Kevin, founder of Glendalough in County Wicklow, was similarly aristocratic. Indeed, Columbanus was relatively high-born. With the monasteries performing social and political functions, it was important for their prestige and status that they were located in accessible places, often along rivers or beside main roads. The early Christian abbot St Cronán moved his monastery to Roscrea, saying, 'I will not be in a desert place where guests and poor people cannot easily find me, but I will settle here in a public place.' He got his wish – now the Dublin to Limerick road runs straight over his chapel.

So it was perhaps appropriate that one of my targets the next morning, the sixth-century monastery of Monasterboice, sits on a hill north of Drogheda, near the route of the new motorway. Even now it offers some insight into the monastic life during Columbanus's time. Ordained brothers lived there (Columbanus was one): they kept the eight monastic offices of the day, and followed a devout, contemplative life. There were also lay brothers, who worked on the extensive lands of the monastery and could marry. With the teaching of the ordained monks, and the craftsmanship of the lay brothers, such monasteries would have been more like small towns than silent retreats. In fact, they were the closest thing Ireland had to towns until the Vikings arrived in their longships several hundred years later (it's no coincidence that all the largest towns in Ireland are near the sea). Monasteries also provided hospitality to travellers, and as Columbanus was travelling north to Bangor, it's possible that he would have stayed at Monasterboice – but as Greg at Newgrange would say, 'That's just speculation.'

It was hard to forget that monasteries were busy places when three coaches were parked outside the entrance. German and American tourists were clambering around what is now little more than a churchyard, enclosed by a circular stone wall with a high tower jutting into the sky. The real draw is the two ninth-century high crosses that stand out among the many gravestones from the last two centuries. These intricately carved stone crucifixes are around eight feet tall, and were built to explain religious stories to an illiterate population, acting as permanent cartoon Bibles. The tourists were queuing up to take pictures of them, but when everyone had got back on to their coaches, I grabbed a couple of minutes alone in the place, trying to catch some sense of it.

When I got back to the entrance, the grey-haired care-taker was leaning on his rake admiring my bike. We chatted a little about my trip.

'You're like my daughter, always travelling,' he said.

'Is that right?'

'She's never home. It's like she'd rather be anywhere else. She was in India. Terrible country. Well, you know yourself.'

'I always thought I'd quite like to go there.'

'Oh, but the crowds and the poverty and the bad food. Would be a terrible place to ride a bike, for a start.'

He had a point. I wouldn't like that very much. Pootling through France and Italy seemed hard enough to me. I'd leave India for the time being.

Where Monasterboice is towers, crosses and modern gravestones all jumbled together, nearby Mellifont is all straight lines, space and coherence. It's tucked away in a shallow valley, and even its name is lovely – from the Latin '*fons melis*', meaning 'fountain of honey'. Founded in 1142, it was the first Cistercian monastery in Ireland, and it follows the classic Cistercian layout, with cloisters surrounding a central grass enclosure. A large octagonal lavabo, or ceremonial wash-basin, stands on one side of the cloisters. As a twelfth-century foundation, it's more than five centuries younger than Columbanus, and was built after Monasterboice had closed, but it represents a French view of monasticism deep in the Irish countryside, making it a mirror image of what Columbanus achieved with Irish foundations in France.

Mellifont also underlined the gap in time between Columbanus and myself – if this abbey was built five hundred years after Columbanus died, and is still so damn old, then there really was a lot of time between us. I pictured myself in France, riding into each of the towns on my list and being confronted by nothing but tower blocks. 'Move along, there's nothing to see here.'

The seaside town of Termonfeckin wasn't exactly on my way, but it deserved a visit for its great name. It's a small place set back a little from the sea so, after stocking up with food at the only shop in town, I rode out to the beach and lunched on the long wide strand. Then I was back on the bike for the trip northwards along the coast through Clogher Head and Annagassan. I was riding through the narrow strip of land between the Dublin–Belfast road and the sea, and it felt strangely forgotten as I drifted along on empty roads, looking at the view across the bay towards the Mourne mountains.

I rejoined the main road in Castlebellingham. Traffic normally thunders through the place, but when I arrived it seemed remarkably quiet. It was a Wednesday afternoon, so I figured the rush hour hadn't started yet. I consulted my map and plotted a route that took me on back roads straight to the village I was heading for to stay with my aunt and cousins. I'd not gone far when the road surface disintegrated, then gave out. Across a fence, across half a field, I saw a motorway. So that was where all the traffic was. I turned around and went the long way to my aunt's house, past the Xerox plant on the edge of Dundalk.

Aunt Nuala had some questions for me. A no-nonsense primary-school teacher, she was happy to see me but wanted to get a few things straight.

'I was talking to my mother about your trip and she wanted to know were you very holy?'

'I don't think so.'

'So you're not doing this for St Columbanus exactly. It's not a devotion?'

'Not really.'

'But it is a pilgrimage?'

'Um . . .'

'And was Columbanus the one who went to Iona?'

At last, a question I could answer. 'No, that's Columba – similar name, different saint.'

'So why *are* you doing this, then?'

I couldn't tell her because I didn't know. I wasn't at all holy. I'd been brought up in a godless household, and only went to church for weddings, funerals and a Christmas sing. If I had been looking for a saint to fix on, there were certainly more attractive ones than the stern Columbanus. His instructions describe how 'the chief part of the monks' rule is mortification . . . let him not do as he wishes . . . Let him come weary to his bed and sleep walking, and let him be forced to rise while his sleep is not yet finished.' Even by the standards of the day, Columbanus enforced a harsh rule over his charges (forty days' punishment if the host got a worm in it on your watch), and he also attacked popes and kings for their lack of piety. Columbanus was a hard-ass, and I was scared of him.

So why was I following him to Italy? Yes, I wanted to do a long trip on the bike, and I was interested in the period. But I had to admit I was surprised at myself. It was one thing to come up with the idea, but now I found myself riding to places on the bike it was all starting to become very real.

4

Northern Exposure

The next morning, I was riding through the bandit country around Forkhill and Jonesborough to avoid the main road into Newry.

A succession of small hills brought me towards the border, and as I slogged up another climb I saw a checkpoint ahead. It was the summer when there had been confirmed cases of foot-and-mouth disease in the North, and one in the Republic, so the police had set up a comprehensive system of checkpoints on border roads to stop the smuggling of livestock. There had initially been huge delays on the major routes, with stories of the gardaí confiscating people's shopping, and I was prepared to reveal whether or not I had any ham sandwiches in my panniers. As always, I felt guilty passing a policeman, even though I knew I hadn't done anything wrong. Or maybe I had, and I couldn't remember. As it was, the overweight round-faced guard stayed leaning against his car and said, 'Good man, not far now.'

As I drew level with him I acted as if I was about to collapse, blowing out my cheeks and rolling from side to side on the bike. People seem to like that.

'It's hard work, but it'll be worth it when you get there,' he observed. How did he know where I was going? Maybe my arrival at the border had been spotted by one of the large observation posts on the northern side, and complex profiling algorithms had determined that I was exactly the sort of character to be riding to Newcastle in pursuit of a long-dead saint. Or maybe he was a Zen guard, for whom destination was less a geographical location than a spiritual sense of well-being. 'It's hard work, but it'll be worth it when you get there.' Wise words, especially to a touring cyclist.

Aside from receiving religious instruction from Sensei Sergeant O'Shaughnessy, there are two other ways you can tell you're going over the border on a back road, according to a friend of mine from Monaghan. Either there's a white box painted on it, so British army helicopters can tell exactly where they are, or you come to a wide, well-surfaced stretch on an otherwise unremarkable road.

'So how do you know that's the border?' I asked naïvely.

'Because that's where it was blown up, and had to be resurfaced.'

'Oh, I see.'

As I rode into Forkhill I was in a spaghetti western – no wonder they called it bandit country. The streets were deserted and a bell was ringing from the whitewashed Spanish-style church – it was high noon. I rounded a corner and almost ran straight into a British army patrol. One soldier was up ahead, kneeling beside a wall with his rifle raised, another was crossing the road in front of me, and a third walking backwards behind him. There had been rioting in Belfast the night before – the worst for months – and although the marching season was some time away, the province was tense. Forkhill, like most of the towns and villages around it, is a staunchly nationalist area, announced by the Irish tricolour flying over the town, so those young soldiers can't have felt too comfortable. But they weren't interested in me, and I cycled through the increasingly hilly terrain past Slieve Gullion and down into Newry.

A quick map check told me my next stop was a place called Hilltown, which sounded like a bad idea. But if I was going to make it over the Alps later in the summer, I shouldn't moan about some Irish uppage first. To prove I wasn't scared, I headed out of Newry up the wrong hill, and had to go down and start again. Lunch was a picnic bought at a petrol station, which is a little like a cow shopping at a butcher's, but I was soon up in the hills, with boy racers zooming past me on the good Nordy roads.

I was in fine cycling form, and enjoying the views as the mountains rose up to my right. As it turned out, it was downhill through Hilltown – 'Gateway to the Mournes' – and the scenery kept getting better.

Just before the road drops down towards Newcastle in County Down, there's a beautiful village called Bryansford. It nestles in the forest, in a quiet but sturdy way, and I imagined myself living there in a stone house with my mountain bike parked out the back. Much better than Dublin. Then I heard the sound of bagpipes and, in the well-manicured front garden of a small house, saw a trim grey-haired man standing in his slippers playing to himself and the trees. I'd have to watch out for the neighbours.

Newcastle is perfectly situated between the sea and the mountains, and I liked it at once. As you come down the main drag, the brooding top of Slieve Donard is lined up like a landscape painting at the end of the street. Drop down to the beach, and you've got a view of the broad bay and the dunes towards the Royal County Down golf course and the Victorian towers of the Slieve Donard Hotel. As the friendly landlady at the B&B said, 'I go for a walk every morning, but actually it's two walks. It's sand and water on the way out, and mountains and trees on the way back.'

For a seaside resort in June it was quiet. Young girls sat behind the counters in the empty ice-cream parlours, and the noise from the amusement arcades had a hollow ring to it. I was staying in a three-storey terrace across the road from the seafront. After my hilly adventures I was happy to grab a shower, then stretch out on the bed and watch some kids' TV.

That evening I walked the length of the path along the beach and doubled back to Diamond Pat's, the restaurant the landlady had recommended. It was upstairs above a deserted pub, and there were only three other sets of diners. There was a young Eurocouple by the window and an older pair over to one side who looked English or Irish. Near the window were a group of sturdy American golfers, who seemed too big for the surroundings.

I'd broken the first rule of solo dining – bring something to read – so I ate quickly and went for a post-prandial stroll. It was after ten and still bright as I sat on the low wall between the beach and the wide path beside it. Two teenage girls were playing tennis on the path a little way along. When one hit the ball over the wall on to the beach they coaxed their little dog to jump down the six feet to retrieve it. The tired-looking terrier wasn't convinced about this plan, but eventually was persuaded to throw herself off the wall. Each time she returned more slowly.

The next morning I came down to breakfast to discover that, except the American golfers, everyone sitting in the

restaurant the night before was now sitting in the breakfast
room waiting for their fry-ups. Either their landlady was on
commission from Diamond Pat, or we were the only visitors
in Newcastle. The young couple were Dutch, and were
driving around the whole island, having arrived in Cork. The
older people were from the Tyneside Newcastle, and on their
way to a wedding in Ballina.

Soon my Ulster fry arrived, and prompted a delay in the
conversation. A cooked breakfast down south might consist
of bacon, sausages, fried egg, tomato and black and white
pudding, with beans or mushrooms if you were lucky. I was
now looking at all of that, plus potato cakes and soda farls.
Add in the obligatory toast, brown bread and a gallon of tea
and I was at once delighted and quietly disgusted at the
amount of food I was going to consume.

Since my days of living in hippy, health-conscious San
Francisco I theoretically didn't eat meat, but on my return to
Ireland I'd had to amend my rules a little in the face of these
beguiling breakfasts. I knew that bacon sandwiches had been
the downfall of better fish-eating vegetarians than I, so I
decided that appeasement was the best policy. Now I didn't
eat meat unless that meat was a pork-based breakfast item
and it was before midday. The rule made no sense, but I
didn't care, and this breakfast was a great one. The bacon
was thick with a crispy rind, the sausages well cooked and
slightly spicy, the mushrooms moist and firm. The runny
egg yolk mixed with the sauce from the baked beans and
soaked into the bottom of the potato cake, while the gently
fried soda farls were crisp on the outside but doughy within
– much like my arteries were going to be.

When I'd eaten enough to slow down a little, I started

talking to the English couple about my trip. They asked the same question Nuala had put to me – 'Is your saint the one who went to Iona?' It's unfortunate that across such a distance of time we're asked to recall two saints with similar names who both left Ireland to found monasteries in the same part of the sixth century. Columbanus just means 'little dove', and is the Latin diminutive of Columba, and it's likely that in reality they were both called Columba to their faces. (Although you'd probably have been better advised to call Columbanus 'Sir' if you didn't want a beating.)

Columba, or Columcille ('the dove of the Church') as he's widely known in Ireland, founded the monastery in Derry, then became involved in the first recorded copyright trial in history. He is supposed to have copied a psalter without its owner's permission. The case came to trial before the local king, with the decision going against Columba: 'To every cow her calf, to every book her copy.' When the monk refused to hand over his copy, things quickly became less than polite, with Columba and his family defeating the king in battle. Under a cloud, Columba was ordered to leave Ireland. He settled on Iona, a small island off Mull on the west coast of Scotland, and founded a monastery there, which was to become crucial in the Christianisation of much of Scotland and northern England, with sister foundations at Melrose, Lindisfarne and elsewhere. Iona also became important politically, with many kings of Scotland buried there (including the original Macbeth). At the time it was on a major route between northern Ireland and the Irish kingdom of Dal Riada in western Scotland, but now it seems extremely remote and is home to a multi-denominational Christian community.

My friends from the other Newcastle had visited the island.

'It's a lovely place, so peaceful,' said the woman, who did most of the talking for the two of them. 'We went to see John Smith's grave.'

My mind tumbled briefly until I connected the name to the former leader of the Labour Party in Britain.

She went on, 'His gravestone lies flat on the ground, because of the weather, I suppose, and it just says on it, "John Smith – an honest man". It brought tears to us eyes.'

It struck me that there aren't many politicians whose deaths would be met with tears from ordinary people. In fact, a few would need to follow John Smith's example with a flat gravestone to allow for all the dancing.

The ride out of Newcastle was uneventful, but arriving in Newtonards I had a problem. I was making good time, and the sun was even breaking through, but the direct route to Bangor was along a dual carriageway – perfect for speeding cars, but not for dawdling cyclists. I had to go out of my way along the ridge to the east of the town to a back route to the coast.

Where Newcastle has an air of slightly neglected grandeur, Bangor is a buzzing seaside town with a marina framed by Victorian villas. The afternoon sun was sharp as I pushed the bike down the main street and out to the sea-front. I'd made it to the first location in which I could definitely place Columbanus – he'd spent over twenty years at Comgall's abbey here.

Abbey Street is the main route out of town to Belfast and Newtonards, but on one side of the road there is a large expanse of parkland that stretches round to Castle Park

Road, and includes the impressive Jacobean-style town hall. Reading in libraries in Dublin and gathering up the kit for the bike had been fun, but now I had ridden 290 kilometres to walk across grass where Columbanus had walked 1400 years before. He'd been an idea, a reason for going, and a focus for historical interest, but this was the first time I'd thought of him as a real person.

In the accounts of most medieval saints' lives, loyal hagiographers describe them as being marked for greatness early on, and Columbanus was no different. While his mother was pregnant with him she had dreamt she 'saw the sun rise from her bosom, and issuing forth resplendence, furnish great light to the world'. If you became a plumber after that kind of entrance, it would be a bit of a let-down. Fortunately Columbanus was a keen student, and Jonas says 'his fine figure, his splendid colour and his noble manliness made him beloved by all', which caused problems. These came in the form of 'lascivious maidens whose fine figure and superficial beauty are wont to enkindle mad desires in the minds of wretched men'. Columbanus recognised the challenges to his piety and devotion, and sought the advice of a female hermit. She told him that if she hadn't been a woman, she 'would have crossed the sea and chosen a better place among strangers as my home', and she encouraged him to 'flee from corruption'. It was into the Church that he fled, but he clearly never forgot her encouragement to travel overseas.

The gradual Christianisation of Ireland is a remarkable story. Since Ireland had never been conquered by the Romans, its social and cultural framework when Christianity arrived was entirely Irish, the patchwork of small kingdoms matched by a wider sense of Ireland as a single cultural unit. There were many different tribes, but there was one language and one set of legal customs. With no Roman influence, there were no towns or even coins, but there was a highly developed oral tradition of myths, place-name histories and poetry. By the mid-sixth century the rest of Europe had seen the collapse of the Roman Empire, and wave after wave of barbarians arriving to loot and pillage as outlined in the *How to Be a Barbarian* handbook. The Italian Jonas reflects wistfully that Ireland was 'charming, productive and free from the wars which trouble other nations'. In this stable environment there had been no place for writing, so the arrival of the written word with Christianity was a perfect manifestation of those lines from the Gospels, 'In the beginning was the Word, and the Word was with God, and the Word was God.'

The very act of writing was a holy thing, since you learnt Latin only to study the holy texts. It is no wonder that early Irish monks were so devoted to grammatical works: on a practical level, they needed all the help they could get with a language they were all learning from scratch; on a more spiritual level, few people in history had such a strong sense of the sanctity of the written word. That reverence for words is clearly seen in the wondrous beauty of the illuminated Gospels such as the Book of Kells that came later as the highest expression of Irish monasticism's respect for the word as God.

To go back to the beginning, the popular story about the conversion of Ireland is that St Patrick arrived at some point in the mid-fifth century and did the whole job on his own, then drove out the snakes, founded Paddy's Day and created green beer. However, this isn't the whole truth. There were undoubtedly Christians here before St Patrick. In 431, a French chronicle records, a bishop called Palladius was sent from Auxerre to minister 'to the Christians in Ireland'. We've no information on what he found when he arrived but, given that pagan customs continued long into the seventh and eighth centuries, it's fair to say that Christianisation was a gradual process, marked by flexibility and the continuation of many older practices. You don't have to look much further than a modern Irish wedding for a perfect example of this combination – the patina of Catholic orthodoxy at the service, and the devoutly pagan excess of the average reception.

The early Irish Church might originally have been based around a network of bishops, but since there weren't any towns to speak of, this structure of metropolitan sees was not really suited to the country. The idea of a monastic family meshed more closely with the localised and tribal nature of the society, and by the time of Columbanus's birth in around 550, it was the abbots who ran things.

One of the remarkable things about the monasteries was their fidelity to the Rome of the Catholic Church, and to the Rome of classical Latin. Columbanus writes in a Latin that is elegant and grammatically correct, and he continually asserts his commitment to the Pope. As he says, 'For all we Irish, inhabitants of the world's edge, are disciples of Saints Peter and Paul, and of all the disciples who wrote the sacred canon of the Catholic faith.'

Columbanus was first taught by a holy man called Sinell, possibly on Lough Erne, but he soon travelled to Bangor and remained at Comgall's monastery for over twenty years.

Comgall's Rule was described as *'stricta, sancta, sedula'* – strict, holy and zealous. It was this model that he would follow when composing the Rules for his own monasteries in France and Italy.

The abbey at Bangor would have been a set of wooden buildings enclosed by a fence and embankment, but now there's nothing to see from the period. There is a stretch of ruined wall from the twelfth century, when St Malachy brought the Augustinian Rule to Bangor. The plaque on the wall comments that he 'travelled widely on the continent and began a magnificent stone church similar to those he had seen abroad'. While that's true, it is a shame there's no mention of another son of the monastery who travelled equally widely on the Continent. But it was Columbanus's curse not to have returned to Ireland, so he's more widely known abroad than at home. There's not even a street named for him in the town where he spent over twenty years. The current abbey church stands near the chunk of wall: it was largely rebuilt in the seventeenth century, then extended in the nineteenth and early twentieth, by which time it had become one of the parish churches for the town. In 1960 a mural was completed as a replacement for the east window. It shows Comgall receiving Christ's missionary command, 'Go ye into all the world . . .'

Walk round the mound of the old castle and stand in front of the current town hall, and there's a view down the hill towards the sea. On the left you can see towards Carrick-fergus on the other side of Belfast Lough. But come out of the harbour and turn right, as Columbanus did in 590 or 591, and you're heading east, then south, away from Ireland towards the rest of the known world.

The nautical theme continued with my meal that night. It was Friday, and the first couple of places I tried were full, so I ended up in the madly busy Lord Nelson's restaurant facing the marina.

'There's room if you'll be out by eight thirty,' I was warned, as the hassled waiter showed me to my table in the corner of the mezzanine level. The items of ship's paraphernalia around the walls hadn't prepared me for the full horror of the laminated menu. Should I have the Captain's Platter, the Pieces of Eight, or perhaps Mutiny on the Bounty? Why the pasta with salmon dish was called the Fletcher Christian I'll never know, but I put aside my pride and ordered it. At the table beside me, the tweed-clad middle-aged man with watery eyes had to ask for a pan-fried Yo Ho Ho while his wife looked on with scarcely concealed contempt.

Out by the marina a woman with big hair and a microphone was leading a group of people in a line-dancing lesson in the evening sun. Mothers wearing sequined Wranglers were trying to get their kids to turn in the right direction, but a four-year-old girl was so swamped by her Stetson that she couldn't see anything. She just stood there while everyone stepped and clapped around her. A crowd had gathered to watch, and I couldn't work out if they were waiting for their turn or couldn't believe what they were seeing. The music was cranked up loud to cover the noise of the petrol generator for the PA, and grandmothers were hooking their thumbs into the belt-loops on their jeans and giving it loads when the generator broke down.

I walked past the boats and out round the headland, mingling with families, kids on skateboards, and teenagers canoodling on the benches. The planners of the rows of Victorian terraces that ring the harbour had shown the good sense to route the roads to the back of the houses, so there was nothing but garden and footpath between the front doors and the sea. It seemed a long way to Bobbio, but at least I'd made a start.

5

Bee-Stings and Ferries

My trip to the North had been at the end of June, and I frittered away July and half of August drinking coffee in various Dublin cafés, pretending I was preparing for the longer journey. In fact, there was little I had to do. The ride to Bangor had shown that I could cover around eighty kilometres a day without much trouble, and as there was only room in my panniers for a limited amount of kit, packing wasn't going to take long.

But maybe I had baggage of a different sort. People kept asking me why I was doing the trip and my stock answers ('Paul Weller told me to' and 'Because it's there') didn't impress anyone. My real motivation was becoming clearer to me, but I felt uncomfortable telling someone I was only doing this adventurous thing because I didn't want to get a real job.

I'd worked in various offices since I left college, and I'd never got over the horror I felt from the beginning. My first job was with the company newspaper for one of the newly privatised water companies in the UK, writing a lot of articles about sewage treatment plants. I'd only just started work and my career was going down the toilet. Most of our headlines were cringingly obvious – any new plans were titled 'In the Pipeline' or 'Bubbling Under' and any social gathering got the 'Water Night!' treatment.

But worse than the work was the realisation that I was selling my time, not my skills. I knew, with crushing certainty, where I'd be from nine until six every weekday for the foreseeable. If I was busy I had to stay late, but there was no going home early if things were slack. I couldn't work out how anyone managed to live a normal life when they were at work all the time. Why were the shops open during the week when nobody with any money could use them? And when were you supposed to do your washing, or buy food, or sit around in cafés with your friends?

After a year, I escaped to Dublin to do a masters degree, and found the student life much more to my liking, but soon I was thwarted again. I needed to work to get money to do all the things I'd never had time to do when I was working. Like many people in Dublin in the mid- to late-nineties, I ended up working for a technology company. I got the job specifically because I knew nothing about technology, which confirmed my theories about the madness of the corporate world. The company produced training courses on using simple word-processors and spreadsheets, and they were looking for a writer who could explain what to do without being too technical or using any jargon. I was perfect because I couldn't be technical and didn't know any jargon. I became the acceptable face of technology, acting as a conduit between people who knew too much, and people who knew too little.

But after seven years and four jobs, I was a man of leisure again, thanks to the bizarre extravagances of the high-tech boom. I cashed in my options when they were still worth something, and was free to do whatever I liked for a while. But removed from the routine of going to work and grumbling about going to work, I wasn't at all sure what I did like.

All I knew was that I wasn't the sort of person who was supposed to work in an office all day, but that pretty much describes everyone. I'd done some freelance journalism in the past, but that didn't grab me. I wondered about radio documentaries, and bought some nice kit to play around with, but then I remembered that I don't really like talking to strangers, so that was out. To have quit my job to write a novel seemed too much of a cliché, but maybe there was some other sort of writing that was better suited to my unlikely skills. Maybe I was the sort of person who followed medieval monks across Europe on a bike. It had the right mix of geeky and cool, and even if I didn't turn out to be a travel writer, the trip might help me work out what I did want to do. That way, I got out of Dublin for a while, avoided working in an office and postponed having to make any more substantial decisions about my life. Perfect.

Meanwhile, my sister was having no such existential problems. The biggest event over the summer was the birth of her and her husband's second child, and I was in London to distract my older nephew and make tea while Uma did all the real work. Although everyone was expecting a baby girl, a huge, hearty boy arrived and was soon outgrowing the newborn clothes that rained on him from friends and family. Soon after the birth Uma was talking to me about names for the child.

'We're thinking of calling him Columbanus as a middle name. Your trip sounds great. What do you reckon?'

Leave him alone, poor little kid, was my first thought, but

fortunately this came out as 'I'm very touched you'd think of that, but isn't "Columbanus" a bit of a burden, even in Brixton where pretty much anything goes? What about Colm – the modern Irish version? Mum would like that.'

Our mother had grown up in Dublin but left when she was eighteen to work in London and then the Channel Islands where she met Dad, a musician at the time. By the time I showed up, the jazzman and the Dublin girl were in leafy Buckinghamshire and, as well as Christmas visits to see the family in Ireland, there were a few hints that our house was not like everyone else's in the street. The family ran on a curious mixture of time zones. Dad was pretty close to GMT but Mum followed Irish time, which had a more flexible way with the passage of minutes and hours. If she said we should leave the house at seven, Dad would be ready at seven, which was always a big mistake – if we made it out the door by eight thirty we were doing well. I grew up with a weird combination of both approaches: I'm normally on time, but I wish I wasn't. And it's useless in Ireland where to arrive on time is to be early.

Another hint that our house was a relaxed Irish enclave was that my school friends were always delighted to come over to play. In true Hibernian style, whoever happened to be there at dinner time got fed, whether Mum had known they were coming or not. By contrast, I'd be round at my mates' houses and would suddenly be told, 'You'll have to go home now. Philip is about to eat,' as if this was a rare and horrible event only to be witnessed by close family and those with the constitution of a Victorian explorer.

There were also the weekends when my parents' friends would gather for parties, and Sunday afternoon would melt into Sunday evening as Robin the drummer laid out newspaper on the dining-room table and got out his brushes. Dad wrapped himself round the double bass that stood in the corner for the rest of the week while he was out doing an uninspiring day job (for a while his employer's tagline was 'The biggest company you've never heard of', which must have been great for employee morale), and another guest would crack open their guitar case, or sit down at the piano. The dining-room carpet got rolled up and my sister and I watched the grown-ups make eejits of themselves to jazz standards. We thought this was what everyone's family did on a Sunday, but then we started watching *Songs of Praise*, and figured out that this probably wasn't so. By the age of ten I'd developed an encyclopaedic knowledge of the songs of Cole Porter and the Gershwins, and Sarah Vaughan was like a godmother to me.

Mum would be pleased if her new grandson was given an Irish name, but going for the full Columbanus seemed unfair to the little chap. I was to blame, as I'd been the one bending my sister's ear about my journey all summer, but I was also aware that it landed me with a degree of expectation. I imagined my nephew Columbanus in years to come saying, 'Yeah, it is a funny name. It's the name of an Irish saint. My uncle was talking about following his journey across Europe, but he only made it as far as Lord Nelson's restaurant in Bangor.'

That didn't sound too good. 'Yeah, it's a weird name but I like it. It's the name of an Irish saint. The summer I was born my uncle rode his bike all the way to Italy tracing Columbanus's route through France and over the Alps,' sounded much better.

So Columbanus ended up as his middle name. I'd have to do it now. For my nephew. Abhisheka Columbanus Dinsmore-Tuli would never forgive me if I didn't.

I'd set out from my street on a bike countless times, and this time didn't feel any different, even if I wouldn't be coming back for months. My friends Paul and Mick had come to see me off on a grey August day, but as I stood at the front door for photos it felt a little fake.

I prepared to lumber down the road. My bags contained everything I thought I'd need: two sets of cycling clothes (plus the set I was wearing), one pair of trousers that zipped off into shorts, three T-shirts, one real shirt, one fleece top, a waterproof and a pair of sandals. All this filled one bag, with all the guidebooks and maps. The other bag contained a tent, a sleeping bag and pad, my toiletries and a charger each for the phone and the camera. My handlebar-bag had all the valuable stuff – digital camera, waterproof mobile phone, tiny shortwave radio, plus that day's map and other documents.

Off the bike, the three bags didn't seem all that heavy, especially as they contained my whole life for the next two months. I'd brought no cooking pots – I didn't want to waste any opportunity to eat well on the road, even when I was camping – so there was no need for front panniers or the added challenge of juggling five bags at the same time. Nevertheless, when Paul tried to lift the loaded bike, he could scarcely get the back wheel off the ground. He'd fancied a spin round the block before I left, but now he decided against it.

'How far are you going on this thing?'

'I reckon it's about 2500 kilometres.'

'Jesus.'

My friends thought I was mad. The non-cyclists couldn't work out how anyone could ride so far on a bike, while the cyclists knew it could be done but weren't sure I was the man to do it. A couple of weeks before my departure, I'd been out for a spin with two of the guys ('spin' being a catch-all term for any bike ride from one mile to a hundred). We'd reached the countryside outside Dublin when I got a puncture. I felt reasonably well prepared – I knew enough never to ride without my pump, tyre levers and spare inner tubes. However, when I started to remove the tyre, my friends couldn't stand to watch my clumsiness and lack of precision. Dave took the wheel and soon had the tube off, so I handed him the box containing a new one. I'd bought the wrong size. Miles produced one of his correctly sized tubes, and Dave examined the tyre.

'This is pretty beaten up, you know. The sidewall's seen better days and there are a lot of cuts. I'd have got a new one a while ago if I were you.'

By this time the lads were reluctant to let me help, so I watched, feeling stupid, while they put in the new tube and pumped it up.

We remounted and set off again. Two hundred yards down the road, the steering turned soggy and I looked down to see another puncture in the same tyre. When we reassembled Miles asked, 'Did you check the inside of the tyre?'

'Sorry?'

Often, whatever caused the puncture is still embedded in the tyre, so the standard practice, I now know, is to inspect the inside of the tyre and remove the offending thorn or shard of glass. I hadn't checked. I let them fix the puncture while I smiled grimly. They were thinking the same thing I was: if I couldn't make it to Swords, how the hell was I going to get to Switzerland?

I said my last goodbyes and trundled down the road to set out on the journey. I tried to concentrate only on today's challenge – through Dublin, then out along the coast as far as Gorey, County Wexford, which was a little over halfway to the harbour at Rosslare, where I had an appointment with a ferry the following afternoon.

It turned out to be a slog of a day. In theory the gradient and the wind should be the only external factors governing your speed on a bike. The road can be narrow, busy or winding and it shouldn't matter: you can be pedalling away at the same speed regardless. But as Yogi Berra said, 'In theory, theory and practice are the same thing. In practice, they're not.' There are fast roads and slow roads for bikes, just as there are for cars, and all the way down I found the slowest roads, with potholes, blind corners and rolling slopes that had ups but no matching downs. In racing cycling, this is known as hard-man country because it favours neither the slight climbers nor the bulky sprinters but stern, mud-caked men from the Low Countries. And even they don't carry panniers.

As I grunted along, I tried to distract myself by listing all the things I thought might go wrong over the next few weeks. I was ill-equipped as far as contingency plans, back-up and mechanical ability went, but if I was mentally prepared for it disaster wouldn't come as a complete surprise. It was obvious: I was going to be lost, wet, robbed, cold, fed up, tired, injured, and very possibly murdered at some point between Dublin and northern Italy, so I'd better get used to the idea. I pictured myself standing at the side of some French road holding several pieces of bike frame while a truck drove past covering me with muddy water. Or emerging from an Italian restaurant to find a blank wall and broken lock where my bike and bags had been.

By the time I'd been robbed at knifepoint on top of an Alp, and had my tent set alight beside the Loire, I'd reached Wicklow Town and stopped for some lunch. I reflected that the biggest issue was travelling alone. That would be the problem if anything serious happened, but even on ordinary days it might prove wearing to be in my own head the whole time. It would be a race to reach Bobbio before I drove myself mad.

Just after Ardmore Point I was stung on the ear by a wasp. I heard a loud buzzing and tried to brush it away, but managed to trap it between the strap of my helmet and my left ear. That hadn't been in my list of likely problems, but I saw it as a sign that I had been right to expect the worst. I'd never been stung, and as I pulled to a stop I convinced myself I was going to die of anaphylactic shock outside a caravan park in Brittas Bay. I dug out my antihistamine tablets and rode off again, waiting for my ear to expand to the size of a wellington boot. By the time I emerged on to the N11 in Arklow, with my ear pretty much its normal size, I figured I was going to live, unless a stray articulated lorry did for me on the run into Gorey.

I'd grumped my way over a hundred kilometres on the first day, which was further than I was planning to ride on any other day of the trip, but I hadn't begun the adventure yet: I was still in Ireland, and Columbanus had definitely not caught the Irish Ferries boat from Rosslare. It didn't help that Gorey is about as delightful as it sounds, so I retired to my room after a big plate of stodge in a near-empty pub, and tried not to think about what six hours of cycling had done to my legs.

Surprisingly, they were fine when I woke up the next morning, and I sped through Enniscorthy, enjoying the wide roads and smooth hard shoulder. Cyclists have to be careful what they listen to just before they head out on their bikes, because there's a good chance they'll find themselves humming it all day. Your mind idles with the rhythmic repetition of the pedal strokes, and there's many an Internet debate on cycling discussion boards about what you should play before you rip up the trails on your dual-suspension, disc-braked steed. Extreme Californian dudes vote for Nine Inch Nails or Limp Bizkit, but riding a touring bike is much more Frank Sinatra than Marilyn Manson so I was singing 'All the Way' and 'From Here to Eternity'.

The rain that threatened all day failed to appear, but Rosslare harbour was still grey and desolate. I lined up with the motorbikes ahead of a queue of cars waiting to board the ferry. The bikers were Italian, German and French, and they stood around introducing themselves and talking away in a mixture of languages, creating a jolly bubble of energy in stark contrast to the people in the cars. The inhabitants of the steel boxes all sat there looking miserable, and wouldn't get out even though it was clear nothing was going to happen for a while. Occasionally a teenager slouched over to the dark ticket office to stock up on Coke and sarcasm. The parents knew they were looking at the thick end of two weeks' uninterrupted family bliss. Meanwhile the Eurobikers admired each other's machines and told motorbike jokes.

I needed all the good humour I could get: I hate boats. I

hadn't been on a ferry since a particularly foul crossing of the Irish Sea on New Year's Day about seven years earlier. I get seasick, and that night I'd been nursing a huge hangover from seeing in the new year with a group of friends that included a gay Italian dressed in a sailor suit. The seas were rough and I was soon hunched over in the quietest lounge trying to convince myself I wasn't there. More and more people started arriving and the noise level increased. I was by turns feverish and chilled, and sweat leached out of my poisoned pores, but I didn't dare open my eyes to find out why there'd been a sudden influx of people. When the film started I twigged I was in the cinema. I was sick, went into a fitful doze, woke in time to be sick again while someone on the screen I wasn't watching said, 'It's Groundhog Day!' I slept again, and woke up to hurl at what seemed to be the same scene in the film. 'It's Groundhog Day!' I was stuck in seasick limbo.

By the time I was reduced to retching into empty crisp packets, death seemed preferable to spending another infinitely recurring minute in that lounge with a film that kept on saying 'It's Groundhog Day!' I vowed then that I would never again take the ferry home. I also get airsick, but the plane journey only takes an hour and you don't have to go through Holyhead.

So, I was taking no chances on the overnight crossing to Brittany. I'd booked a berth so I could be ill in private, and was dosing myself up with Dramamine, the weapons-grade travel-sickness tablet that I'd relied on for all my flights in the States. I eschewed the herbal remedies and non-drowsy formulas for the extra-drowsy, extra-strength napalm of the nausea world. It took me a night's sleep to recover from the tablets each time, so I can't remember what happened on the business trips I took, but I was never ill.

I rode up the slippery metal ramp into the guts of the ferry, and lashed my bike to a bit of metal as if it was going to be tempted by Sirens. I could feel the drug beginning to work.

No matter how you dress it up, a ferry is an ugly thing, with a feel somewhere between a barracks and a 1950s hospital. The fresh paint and subdued lighting of the restaurant are betrayed by the metal walls and the lifeboats outside the windows. But I didn't care about much as I lay dozing in my tiny cabin (it's not often you can touch three sides of a room that doesn't have a toilet in it). The Dramamine had put my head in a Perspex box. The outside world seemed a long way away, and I lay there listening to a radio report about thieves who had stolen a chunk of the wall from the quays alongside the Liffey in Dublin. But that might have been the drugs talking.

I hardly stirred from my horizontal position for the sixteen hours of the crossing, and kept myself topped up with tablets so I didn't wake to find their effect wearing off. In the morning I emerged to eat some breakfast I couldn't taste as land came into view. The ferry was docking at Roscoff, out on the western tip of Brittany, but history has Columbanus and his followers landing near St Malo, a long way further east. The first few days of my French riding would be through areas without much of a Columbanian connection. However, I'd found a reference to a church dedicated to him in a tiny village inland near Pontivy, which was to be my target the next day. First I wanted to get a few kilometres behind me before my first night's camping.

I joined the drivers on the car decks and rode down the ramp out into the small port. Trying to remember to ride on the right, I negotiated my first French roundabout and was soon heading along a quiet coast road, having given the big traffic the slip. My Michelin map was in its case at the top of the handlebar-bag, I had chewy cereal bars, full water-bottles and I felt that the trip had really begun. The road from Morlaix was empty, perfectly paved and picturesque as it meandered through a wooded river valley for nearly an hour. An old guy dressed in the colourful kit of the Dutch cycling team Rabobank eased past me on a shiny bike, but that was almost all the traffic I saw.

As the afternoon wore on I began to slow down as the road left the valley and started to climb a series of hills. So far I'd drifted through the day, my legs spinning under me without effort, but this was hard and I grimaced my way up the last climb. I stopped for supplies in a supermarket on the edge of the town of Huelgoat, then sped down a steep hill and stopped in front of a run of bars, restaurants and souvenir craft shops beside a lake. Wait a minute, I've been here before, I thought.

Just after I left college, in an earlier attempt to avoid making a decision about my future, I'd taken a holiday driving around Brittany, and had read about the 'Roche Tremblante'. I'd pictured an inverted triangle of rock that you could tilt with your little finger. I'd arrived at the location and chased along past elderly Frenchwomen on the steep and narrow paths, but was brought up short when I reached the rock. It was a huge slab, shaped like a giant pillow, and it lay flat on the ground. A game German put all his weight into a shove, and a crowd waited to see the rock move, but it was a huge let-down. It was in Huelgoat, where I was going to spend my first night in France.

This time I had more pressing needs than seeing a rock tremble. I was feeling dizzy, and my legs didn't want to work any more. I found the campsite on the other side of the lake, and leant my bike against a stone pillar, then headed into the registration shed. The weight of the panniers promptly pulled it backwards round the pillar and the crossbar ground against the stone. Now there were two nasty grooves scratched into the paintwork. Lovely.

All I wanted was a shower and a lie-down, then some food, but first I had to unpack the gear and put up the tent. It was supposed to be idiot-proof – there was a long pole, a short pole, the tent itself and the flysheet, but I had great difficulty assembling them into anything that you could sleep in. Not counting the pegs, there were just four working parts, but it took me the best part of an hour to get them to play nicely together. So far, I'd ridden for three days and ended up in pieces at the end of two. The Dramamine probably hadn't helped, but this didn't augur well for the rest of the journey.

Another bad pattern that had emerged was my failure to eat a decent evening meal. The big fries in the North had distracted me from the mediocre evening fare, and I'd not expected great things in Gorey or on the ferry, but here was a chance to put things right. I walked back to town and found a place with a busy dining room overlooking the lake. I went in, and was ushered insistently into the dark bar where they put sad solo diners. For some reason I decided I should mark my arrival in France with a pizza. It was only bogging. Amorphous pale artichoke hearts and plastic mushrooms sat on rubber cheese, but it was huge and I was ravenous so I ate it, then walked back in the gloaming to work out how my kit and I were supposed to fit into the tiny tent.

I had three bags to stash into a space so small that if you didn't sleep motionless flat on your back you'd be sure to touch the sides. Imagine yourself lying in an open coffin. Put your arms straight up in the air, and imagine someone draping a sheet over them from above so that it drops down to the edges of the coffin. That was about the size of the tent – I was sleeping in a bright yellow coffin. After much shuffling of panniers, shoes and the handlebar-bag, I carved out enough space to lie down.

I had some vivid dreams, but I woke with the satisfying feeling of being simultaneously comfortable and adventurous for having slept in a tent. Outside the mist was so dense that I couldn't even see the lake about forty metres away, and while it hadn't rained, the flysheet was soaking wet from the damp mist. Although I felt better for the rest, I was still slow in packing and getting ready to go. Across from me, a serious-looking Dutch guy was running a supertechnical squeegee affair over his taut dome tent to dry the flysheet. All I could remember from primary-school camping trips to Dorset was that it was a Very Bad Thing to put a tent away wet. I waved the flysheet around a bit, but it made no difference and I soon gave up. The well-equipped Netherlander looked shocked as he saw me folding the damp tent over on itself and shoving it into the bag. He knew what punishments the Camping Furies would unleash on me for this crime, but I didn't and I had places to go.

6

Spinning through Brittany

Brittany looked like Louth, but the shuttered stone houses and the ubiquity of Renaults assured me that this was France. That, and all the people speaking French.

Until I'd lived in the US, I'd never identified myself as a European. Depending on the circumstances I'd either be English or Irish (which was handy if a little disruptive to one's sense of self), but I was never 'European'. But when I'd met Italians, Spaniards or Germans in America, it was clear how much we shared in terms of values and histories. We all came from a football-mad continent full of towns with many centuries of different buildings, and showers that were too weak. We'd been involved in each other's bloody histories for millennia, and we all knew about Michael Schumacher and the Eurovision Song Contest. It might not seem much to go on, but it had been a comfort while I was stranded in Kansas, a thousand miles from the nearest sea.

My thigh muscles were tender leaving Huelgoat, but the first ten kilometres were largely downhill, and the sun had begun to come out. After a couple of hours I found myself on an exposed uphill stretch of dual carriageway with a glass-strewn hard shoulder, thinking how difficult it all was. This clearly wasn't a holiday – it was a job. Not a job with voicemail and dress-down Friday. This was real work.

Around noon the traffic on the busy road eased as everyone stopped for lunch, and I pressed on into the small town of Rostrenen. Yesterday's weakness might perhaps have been due to lack of fuel, and I'd already notched up around forty kilometres that morning, so I wasn't going to hold back in the cheerful restaurant I found. A smart young man in a suit was sitting at one table, across from a group of builders at another. I sat down in my Lycra shorts and shiny top, and no one batted an eyelid. It was great to be in a cycling country. Soon my pork escalope arrived. I'd been in France barely twenty-four hours and I'd already abandoned any pretence about not eating meat. I felt somehow that if I was going to do such a basically physical activity as ride a bike all day, I wanted to eat flesh. Then I had a large slice of chocolate cake and a small intense cup of coffee. My body was in charge now, and my mental state was directly related to how much I'd eaten in the previous hour. For someone who had made his living in the vapourware world of the Internet, where nothing had a material existence, this concentration on the physical was going to take some getting used to. Right now my body was telling me that it wanted to sleep in a bed that night, so I called into the tourist office. There, the quietly stylish young woman behind the counter made a reservation for me at the hotel up the road in St Nicolas and asked if I was English. I dodged the issue and told her I lived in Dublin. She smiled broadly. A good answer in Celtic-tinged Brittany.

There was supposed to be a church dedicated to St Columbanus on the road to St Nicolas, and after a few kilometres a sign for 'St Columban' directed me down a narrow lane. My map showed a church round there somewhere, but there was no sign of the lane I was on. I rode off into uncharted territory and was soon on a very rough road. I convinced myself I was lost, but then it widened a little and deposited me in front of a squat grey Romanesque church. It was T-shaped with two small side chapels at the back, and almost no windows. A bell hung in a simple open belfry above the main front door, with a rope dangling down to head height. Across the road I saw a badly worn stone crucifix. There were some figures on the back of the pillar, but it was hard to tell how many, let alone if one was St Columbanus. There was nothing to say he was ever there (it's further east than the spot where he's supposed to have landed), but the fact that the church had been named for him shows he was remembered. It was a quiet, remote spot, and the first place in France that had a definite connection with Columbanus.

St Nicolas is a small town, so it wasn't hard to find the only hotel, in the middle of the main square. The young proprietress helped me wheel my bike round to the back, then asked if I'd be watching TV. I said no, which reduced the price for the night, while leaving the television in the room. A Breton honour code was obviously in force, and when I switched on the TV later to check the weather forecast, I felt guilty. It was good to be back in a real room after the ferry and the tent, and I didn't feel quite so destroyed after the day's riding, so I washed everything I'd worn so far, and rigged up my elastic washing line across the window while I listened to the cricket commentary on the radio. A good job the woman in the tourist office couldn't see me – listening to cricket? Of course I was English.

Dinner downstairs in the hotel was a lavish four-course affair. There was a large family group of English tourists at the table in the window. At one end the two-year-old sat in his highchair beside his sulky five-year-old brother, who only wanted '*le sausage avec les chips*'. At the other end their grandmother was wondering if she was brave enough to order the snails. They all had tans shading to redness on their noses and, apart from the five-year-old, they were a happy bunch.

I should have said hello, but English people abroad (myself included) can be funny about greeting their country-men: they're too busy pretending they're the only Brits with the wit to get on a ferry. Instead, I sat there with my book and looked German. I'd had a severe buzzcut before I left (it was the first time I'd ever walked out of a barber's with exactly what I expected, but it's hard to misinterpret 'Number two all over, please'). With my glasses, my black fleece top and my sandals, my look said young Munich architecture student concentrating hard on enjoying himself.

I woke up the next morning to see the rain sheeting down. I lingered over breakfast, but sooner or later I was going to have to head out. The attentive young landlady offered me bin-bags for my panniers, and I struggled with my schoolboy French:

'*Merci, mais ils sont …*'

'*Imperméables?*'

'*Oui, imperméables, j'espère.*'

I got soaked retrieving the bike, so now I was hoping devoutly that the panniers were indeed waterproof. I hung around in the foyer of the hotel for a long while, and when the rain eased a little I zipped up my jacket and headed out.

My cyclist friend Dave argues, 'There's no such thing as unsuitable weather, just unsuitable clothing.' And even unsuitable bikes. Serious riders in Ireland often have a 'winter bike' with mudguards, which they use in place of their svelte, more expensive racing bike. There's so much debris on the wet roads that the oil on your chain quickly turns to grinding paste, and there's so much spray flying around that without mudguards you can't ride close behind anyone, which you need to do if you're to make any headway against gale-force winds. In the past, cyclists used to get eye infections from the cow dung splattering up from the Tarmac. Now we wear sunglasses with orange lenses (Bono and Ali G stole the idea from us), which have the dual effect of protecting our eyes from flying crap and brightening an iron-grey sky. You can't cycle in Ireland without having an affinity with rain, so once I was out on the bike getting wet, I was fine. The roads were empty and the landscape offered the same rolling hills I'd seen in the first two days, and the kilometres ticked by on the trip computer. I'd started talking to myself: 'There's the first five K,' then 'That's ten K you won't have to do again. Well done, David, well done, bike.'

The rain eased off later in the morning, and I fixed on the picture-book medieval town of Moncontour for lunch. It sat on a rocky crag above a river, with stern walls ringing the steep narrow streets. Brazenly, I left the bike leaning up against the largest building I could find, and went into a crêperie for the trip's first *galette* – a Breton buckwheat-flour pancake with a savoury topping, like a pizza. It had turned apocalyptic outside. The rain was coming down so hard that old women had pulled back their net curtains to watch the water sweep across the square. My panniers were still on the bike, so all my kit was being treated to this high-powered jetwash. Suitable clothing or not, I wasn't crazy, so I stayed put until the strong winds blew the storm past and people started to emerge from their shelters.

Pools of water were lying on top of my panniers when I made it back to the bike. If everything was soaked, there was nothing I could do now, so I picked my way back down the steep lanes to the bottom of the hill and started out for the campsite at Jugon-les-Lacs. It was a straight, quiet road, and as the afternoon wore on the sun appeared for the first time that day. I peeled off my jacket and, as I rode along, experienced a strangely blessed state. My speed rose steadily, my legs were spinning beneath me without any effort, and my mind was cleared of all the normal chatter. I noticed tiny details of the roadside as I sped by. I could have cycled all day like that. In sports psychology this state is called 'flow', when a familiar action becomes so grooved that on occasion it seems to happen of its own volition, often better than you thought you could do it.

Whatever it was, it got me to Jugon, and stopped me worrying about whether my sleeping-bag was soaking wet.

Jugon-les-Lacs was a small, stone-built town gathered around a long central square below a lake. You had to walk up a steep bank to the side of the lake, as if the town was afraid of getting wet. The campsite was about half a mile out of Jugon, much larger than the one at Huelgoat, with a swimming-pool, a bar and two rows of chalets for people who liked more than a canvas roof over their heads. While the visitors near the trembling rock had been largely tourists from England, Holland and Germany who were just passing through, Jugon was a place where French people came for their holidays and there were as many caravans as tents. Squads of kids were chasing around and the reception desk had a computerised check-in system. I had to ride round and find my plot, then report its number to Reception where it was marked off on the onscreen map. Very cool, but a little excessive for a one-night stay in my yellow coffin.

The contents of my fine German panniers were dry, and the tent went up a little more easily than before. Even though I was only riding for five hours a day, all the necessary packing and unpacking, preparing to leave and sorting out on arrival took such a long time that my days were full. As soon as I reached somewhere, all my bags exploded like bottles of Coke that had been shaken up all day. There was stuff everywhere, but what I needed never came easily to hand. Even a trip to the shower with a change of clothes meant sorting through any number of different piles of kit, and I invariably forgot something crucial. Like my towel. The sun had disappeared behind one of the hills beside the lake as I walked back into town. Smart British-registered estate cars, complete with GB stickers and little wedges of black tape on the headlights, were parked in the main square. I chose what looked like a simple enough restaurant and walked in to be confronted by three smart young women in short black skirts, black tights and white blouses.

Did I have a reservation? Er, *non*. They shrugged collectively, and one went to see if there was any room for this scruffy boy in their smart dining room. It was still early, but it was a Saturday night and it was clear that this was the hot ticket in Jugon. The waitress returned and, with a look that said I'd been granted a great boon, led me to a small table surrounded by loud groups of comfortably-off English

Volvo drivers. Travelling alone means you create little disturbance, and can pass through places without leaving a ripple. If you're in a large group the energy and weight of your numbers distort the environment around you, and you end up moving in a cocoon of your own making. And in the case of my fellow diners, this was a little bubble of Home Counties commuter life. One man behind me was talking to his family as if they were in constant need of the wisdom he'd gained from long years of taking the seven twenty-seven to Marylebone and sitting in an office all day. He was at pains to correct his wife and teenage children at every opportunity.

'Well, if you ask me,' and nobody had, 'most of what passes for modern music is unlistenable to. And when some talentless oaf takes a snippet of someone else's song and uses it as his own, that's just criminal. The man can't even play an instrument, how can he be a musician? That's not music …' The teenage staff fetched and carried elegantly prepared dishes of duck and fish for the *rosbif* clientele. I saw none of the people from the campsite, and I realised this was the English visitors' idea of a perfect French holiday: great food and wine, but none of those annoying French people around.

Back at the tent, the French campers were all in party mood. The bar was playing loud Europop (that really isn't music), and the kids were chasing around on bikes in the dark, darting out from around the hedges and running over tent pegs. In surrounding caravans radios were cranked up, and the people next to me were taking their big dome tent down by the light of their car's headlights. Once I was inside mine, it sounded as if legions of people were walking along the nearby gravel path, then turning off to come and stand around discussing whether anyone could be inside such a bizarre-looking thing. It took me a long time to get to sleep, but eventually the glass of kir and half-bottle of wine started to kick in.

French baked goods are the best breakfast a cyclist can have. I'd buy fresh buttery croissants or *pain aux raisins* from the local baker and munch them as I rode along. I chewed my way down the morning back roads, skirting Dinan and heading north-east towards the coast near St Malo. If the ferry from Rosslare had docked there rather than at Roscoff I would have saved myself four days' riding and arrived much closer to the place where Columbanus is said to have landed. But travelling across a large chunk of Brittany was allowing me to get into a routine of riding, eating and sleeping before I reached many places with historical connections to explore.

It was a Sunday, so there were a few more cyclists out on the road, most of them middle-aged guys in full Lycra kit. Professional cyclists have a physique that's seldom seen in the real world – sculpted legs that are tanned and shaved, slim torsos and long, skinny arms. Their bulges are all muscle, and somehow make the Dayglo figure-hugging kit look good. However, when a Breton accountant in his fifties wears the same shorts and jersey, too much is revealed: the pale hairy legs, the roll of fat over the waistband and the wobbles in the upper arms as they go over a bump.

But there's a good reason for wearing this stuff. It improves your comfort markedly if you're on a bike for any length of time. The shorts include chamois inserts to come between you and the saddle, while the jerseys are tight enough not to billow in the wind, and are made of technical fabrics that wick moisture away from the skin, keeping you dry even when you're sweating. There are also pockets sewn on to the back of the jerseys, so you can carry keys, wallets, mobile phones (and croissants) with ease.

I stopped to consult my map, and an older gent on a shining 1980s racing bike pulled up and offered his assistance. He was wiry, grey-haired and tanned, wearing wraparound cycling glasses and last year's Gan team kit. He pointed out the right road to me, and rode off in the opposite direction.

The clouds darkened and it was soon raining hard, so I stopped under some broad trees at the edge of a village to wait for the rain to ease. I started out again, and a little while later was caught by the old màn who had given me directions. He was now wearing a clear plastic racing cape and a cycling cap, but his glasses were still in place and we rode along companionably while he asked me where I was from and where I was going. We spoke the international language of cycling – discussing how far I would ride in a day, whether I had Shimano or Campagnolo equipment on my bike, and which way the wind tended to blow around here. He'd been riding for fifty years, and certainly looked well on it. As we went through a couple of villages he waved to people he knew, then said goodbye and pulled into the driveway of his house. A gentleman cyclist – I hope I'm still going out for my Sunday spins when I'm his age.

He left me with the rain still pouring down, and I picked my way over the motorway, then started going downhill rapidly towards the bridge over the Rance at Port St Hubert.

I'd never managed to adjust my brakes properly, so they weren't great at the best of times, and with rain coming down and up in dirty sheets of spray from the road, I gave the bike her head and zoomed across the narrow bridge with a stupid grin on my mucky face. Once you're wet, you're wet. If you're driving your car and see people out on their bikes in rainy weather, save your pity. It might look unpleasant, but it's more than possible that they're having a great time. Especially when it stops raining and the sun comes out. Then the technical wickable fabrics get to work and you arrive at your destination filthy but dry. So it was that I approached the town of Cancale, which lies across a steeply sloped hill at the west end of Mont St Michel Bay. The centre of town gathers around the church at the top of the hill, and the port area, with fishing-boats and restaurants, at the foot.

After six days' riding, it was time for a break, so I chose one of the small hotels on the front and booked in for two nights. The room was on the side of the building (a drawback of solo travelling is that you never get the big rooms at the front) but if I stuck my head out of the window and looked to the right, I could see the bright blue of the bay, with the sea fading into the sky. Lovely, but it was time for a nap.

While I was asleep, it rained again, and I was happy to be safely tucked up in my little room. It's OK to get wet once in a day, but it's tedious if it keeps happening, and I was off the clock anyway. I ran through a quick ache inventory. I felt in pretty good shape. My yoga-teacher sister had taught me a set of poses and stretches that were supposed to be an antidote to cycling, and I'd been dutifully lying on my back with my legs in the air at the end of each day. As a result, the backache and sore neck I'd feared hadn't materialised, and my knees were still moving smoothly. My thighs felt a little sore, and I winced walking upstairs, but at least I was still walking. The delicate points where I met the saddle of the bike were also tender, but I'd been slathering myself with Sudocrem (a tip I'd picked up from my new nephew), and the ergonomically designed seat seemed to be looking after the guys. I'd not lost anything, fallen off the bike or decided I hated the whole thing and abandoned the project. Pretty good for my first week. But I still felt disaster had only been postponed, not avoided.

7

Brief Encounters

Talking about medieval saints is not sexy. For months, people's eyes had glazed over when I'd launched into a disquisition on hagiography and biblical exegesis. None of the books I consulted in the libraries were ever being used by anyone else when I needed them. I was a lone freak, ignored in my own land. But here in a small village in Brittany I was among friends, like a cross-dresser amid a group of size-twelve slingbacks.

After a morning spent writing postcards and staring across the bay at Mont St Michel peeking from behind the mist, I'd set off for the village of St Coulomb, named for our sailing saint. The sun came out and, without the heavy panniers, the bike felt sprightly as I arrived at a nineteenth-century statue of Columbanus, or St Colomban as he's known in France. He's got a beard, is leaning on a long staff, and has a dove perched on his shoulder. The sun is carved on the front of his robe, and a faint smile plays around his lips. He looks saintly and peaceful, not at all like the stern disciplinarian I knew from his writings. Victorian saints had to be polite and not scare the children.

The parish church is bedecked in Columbanus memorabilia. A painting on the roof of the nave shows a lone grey-bearded saint standing up at the back of what looks like a Viking longship. The sail has a huge Chi-Ro pattern on it, and there's a cross on the prow. A shaft of sunlight from a cloudy sky enfolds our hero in golden light, which he hardly needs as he's sporting a halo of his own. He's holding the tiller in one hand, a Bible in the other, and looks like a monastic action figure. This is much more what I had in mind for Columbanus.

He should look tough because he did an extremely tough thing. In the legal codes of his time, Irish kingdoms had no death penalty, even for murder. The most severe punishment that could be applied was exile. Without the status that came with being known, and tied to your place, you became a non-person. Columbanus and his followers volunteered to align themselves with murderers.

This equation with death is not accidental. The Christian-isation of Ireland was a gradual and peaceful process, which created problems for devout men like Columbanus. They knew that martyrdom was a mark of true faith, but there was no one in Ireland to do you the great service of killing you for your beliefs. Since this 'red martyrdom' was unavailable as an option for aspiring saints, early Irish Christians devised two other career paths. One was to leave your own area and become an ascetic monk in the wilderness – 'green martyrdom' – and many pursued it, like the female hermit who met Columbanus in his youth. But leaving Ireland entirely – 'white martyrdom' – was the more extreme: you became a *peregrinus* – a Latin word that originally meant 'stranger' or 'foreigner', and later 'pilgrim'. In Irish, there were different words to describe a stranger from another kingdom in Ireland, or one from overseas, which showed that when Columbanus arrived on the shore near this church, he'd crossed a line. He was now a *cú glas*, a 'grey wolf', or, in a beautifully expressive term, a *muirchuirthe*, 'one thrown up by the sea'.

There was an exhibition on the saint around the walls of the church, with detailed maps, posters from Austria and Italy, and even a menu from a tea-shop in St Columb Major in Cornwall. Clearly devout Breton parishioners were sent out at intervals to other places with connections to the saint. What I thought of as a grand adventure was little more than a Sunday-school outing for the children of St Coulomb.

Back out in the sunshine I rode through the small village and made for the nearby coast, stopping at the edge of the village to take a self-timed picture: 'Me Standing in Front of Signpost'. It was the first of what was to become an international series. I was on my own, so I needed to be able to prove that I'd been to these places. After turning right at a T-junction on the coast, I soon came to a cross and a stone tablet marking the spot where the angry Irishman had landed his boat fourteen centuries ago. The calvary had been erected in 1892, and in the 1980s a plastic board of information had been added. At the foot of the cross was a small pot of fresh flowers. Across the road on the beach, however, everyone was much too busy catching some rays and cavorting in the sea to pay Columbanus any attention. Kids were clambering over large rocks revealed by the low tide, while their parents half watched from their towels. With the beach enclosed on both sides by low hills, it would have been a good place to land a boat, but with the holidaymakers building sandcastles near me it was difficult to imagine Columbanus striding through the surf on to the beach. But that didn't matter – after a week, I'd reached a place he'd definitely seen.

Seafood was the only game in town in Cancale, and I'd already sized up the dining options the night before – each place had the same menu, you just had to decide how much you wanted to pay. I found a quiet one at the unfashionable end of the main drag. My fellow diners were mainly elderly French tourists, who were cracking, gouging and sucking at a range of unidentifiable crustaceans. One man had an array of implements before him on the table and was dissecting his meal with a surgeon's precision. Soon, the tower of creatures on his right had been turned into a still taller tower of body parts on his left. The signal-to-noise ratio of edible delicacies to unusable carcass must have been tiny. I ordered a seafood salad and chips so I wouldn't have to get too medieval with my dinner, but this was the coward's way out.

I went to bed early, but my plans for a good night's sleep were interrupted by two mosquitoes. In theory, human versus mozzie is hardly a fair fight, given a human's superior size and supposed intellectual advantage. But at three in the morning in a high-ceilinged hotel room with cream walls, an average mosquito can give you a good run for your money. The window was open, and I had been looking forward to gentle sea breezes entering my room as I slumbered. Instead I got the high-pitched whine of two mosquitoes circling my head. No matter how hard you try to ignore them, you know that in the end you're going to be chasing round the room in your boxers trying to splat them with the back of a book. After something of a Pyrrhic victory I shut the window and returned to bed.

The next day the first half-hour of riding was almost perfect. I followed the flat road south along the bay for a time with the sun shining and a constant view across sand dunes to the pale blue water. But then the road turned south towards Dol, and I was met by a steady wind in my face. For the rest of the hot day I struggled into it. It was hardly noticeable when I stopped, but forced more and more effort from my legs when I tried to turn the pedals. Five hours of riding brought me to the tourist office beside the château in Châteaugiron, a small town that's twinned with Manorhamilton in County Leitrim. (How do you get to be twinned with a small town in Leitrim? I imagined blindfolded French mayors sticking pins into a map of Ireland.) Five minutes later I was sweatily checking in at the small municipal campsite, where the overnight fee was less than the price of a pint.

It had been a hard, hot day, unleavened by any sightseeing – I'd just been covering distance, heading south towards the Loire at Nantes. I pitched the tent and was back from my shower when a boy of perhaps eleven rode his bike over to me and started examining the yellow coffin.

'*C'est bizarre, la tente, n'est-ce pas?*'

'*Oui, mais c'est bonne pour moi, parce que je suis en vélo.*'

That was about the limit of my schoolboy French, even when talking to a French schoolboy. I tried to tell him that I'd ridden a hundred kilometres that day, and had come all the way from Dublin, but I don't think he understood. He wasn't really listening, just buttering me up.

'*Peut-être vous pouvez me donner vingt francs?*'

He wanted twenty francs. '*Pourquoi?*'

'*Parce que je veux acheter du pain. Je retournerai votre argent plus tard, quand mon père …*'

In case my old French teacher Miss Munday's reading this, I should stop now. She never taught us the future tense, so I'm just guessing, and there should probably be some conditionals or subjunctives in there as well. I'd grasped that he wanted me to give him some cash, and he'd give it back to me when his dad got home. I wasn't sure if sarcasm translated exactly, but I tried to sound stern: '*Je pense que non.*'

It seemed to work. The kid did a particularly Gallic shrug and rode off. Most of the other campers were French pensioners in caravans, so he might have been waiting all day to shake down some young foreign visitor. It was nearly time to get something to eat, which meant leaving my tent, bike and kit unattended while I went into town. I didn't have a choice. I imagined the kid returning to torch my tent and make off with my panniers. Maybe the pensioners could keep an eye out for the juvenile racketeer while I went to eat.

Châteaugiron has pleasant, winding streets and half-timbered houses, and there were several restaurants in town, but they were all shut. The place felt like a film set when they've stopped shooting for the day. I thought I'd have to go back and eat the emergency energy bars I'd tucked away at the bottom of one of my bags, but then I found an Italian place that was empty but not closed. I went in and consumed a huge bowl of pasta. It had been a working day, so I ate like a workman.

My hoodlet had evidently been sent to bed early and he'd left my stuff intact so I slept well, but woke up feeling stiff and sore. It was to be another day of distance not sights as I headed south.

I was getting quicker at packing up, and was soon in a

main street that was as bustling as it had been empty the night before – I started looking around for the cameras. It was very hot again, but I reached a certain temperature and degree of sweatiness and stayed there on a bearable plateau. By the time I reached my destination, I'd ridden 190 kilometres in two days – less than a Tour de France rider manages in one, but it was more than enough for me.

All day I'd been staring at this smudge of black and white on the map in front of me that bore the name Nort-sur-Erdre. When I got there, and saw all the features I'd identified on the map – the river and the bridge, the church and the town hall – it felt a little like coming home. I'd been sitting in Dublin planning my route when I first spotted the town on the map and marked it as a place to stop, but as I never booked any accommodation in advance I never knew what I was going to get as far as hotels were concerned.

But this being France, even the smallest towns seem to express a pride and confidence that their British and Irish cousins lack. Nort-sur-Erdre might not be that important, but the town doesn't apologise for itself and proudly points the way to its tennis courts, restaurants and other amenities, one of which was the lovely hotel I found. It wasn't grand, and it didn't have a sweeping gravel driveway or a jacuzzi with gold taps in every room, but it was the kind of small family-run inn that just worked well. I wheeled my bike round the side of the building and into a courtyard with parked German and British cars. Madame booked me in while Monsieur opened the door to the garage across the courtyard for my bike. It was part barn and part wine cellar, with flagstones on the floor and the musty smell of decades in the air.

I was shown up to my room at the top of the house at the back. It was small but nicely decorated with a tall, narrow window that looked out over the courtyard and sun-dappled garden. I'd picked up a pile of information magazines in a quick stop at the tourist office and I surveyed the forth-coming attractions. The day before I'd been looking out towards the Channel Islands and Normandy. The following day I'd be beside the Loire in Nantes, then heading down the river towards other towns I'd heard of – Blois, Tours, Angers.

That night there were only three other diners in the smart restaurant downstairs. A lone German man sat reading a magazine and communicating with the cute young waitress in single words. In the corner a sunburnt older English couple were having trouble translating the menu. The waitress helped them out and brought them their kir before coming to me. She was in the industry's standard white blouse, short black skirt and black tights, with her blonde hair pulled back from her face, and had a brisk but friendly manner. She knew I was the *monsieur* who was riding a bike, and asked me where I'd come from that day.

'*Châteaugiron, près de Rennes.*'

'*Alors, c'est loin, n'est-ce pas?*'

Far? Well, it wasn't that far, but it's great that non-cyclists think it takes a lot more effort than it really does to cover a distance of, say, ninety kilometres. I tried a shrug modelled on the kid from the day before, and told her it was fairly far.

'*Très bien, Monsieur.*'

The food was good, but the details and protocol of the service were better: the wine in its ice bucket, a napkin arranged around the neck of the bottle, and the pause before dessert when the waitress arrived with a silver knife on a tray. With a smile and a little flourish, she gracefully swept all the breadcrumbs from the crisp tablecloth and on to the tray. I thought of the frozen chips and goujons of un-identified white fish I'd eaten in Gorey at the end of my first day from Dublin. Nort-sur-Erdre was about the same size town, but here I was enjoying a culinary experience of a different order. And maybe, the wine began to persuade me, the waitress was being nice to me not just because it was her job.

Unfortunately I'm not the most adept at the arts of seduction: I crash and burn in English, so in French I couldn't even get off the ground. When she brought the bill, all I could do was sign the credit-card slip as suavely as possible. Loser. If I was trying out the role of travel-writing adventurer, shouldn't that make me smooth and confident? I imagined myself projecting a rugged individualist charm with a look that said, 'I'm just passing through, but tonight I'm all yours.' In reality, my look seemed to say, 'Slightly shy, well-mannered Anglo-Irish dude with absolutely no chat-up lines.' As a poor consolation, I spoke to the English couple as we headed for our rooms. This was their first time in France, and they'd been driving around the Loire valley. They didn't have much French, but they were keen to try out lots of experiences, so they'd been putting together big picnics by pointing at whatever took their fancy in *charcuteries*. They were reluctant to drive into the middle of cities, so when looking for places to stay, they'd take their chances in the countryside by following signs for *chambres d'hôte*, or bed-and-breakfasts. Last night they'd ended up at a small château and been presented with a bedroom as large as the downstairs of their home, complete with a dressing room and two *en-suite* bathrooms. As they spoke, they looked as if they hadn't bargained for just how different France was.

As we were talking on the landing, the waitress from the restaurant came up the stairs behind us. She flashed another smile as she disappeared along the corridor to her room. With the husband-and-wife team running the place, and a chef working modest wonders in the kitchen, she was perhaps the only other employee. And she was sleeping under the same roof? That wasn't fair.

The next morning I tidied up the explosion of kit that had happened in my room. My radio, phone, wallet and keys were on the bedside table. My tent was drying out, dangling from a corner of the wardrobe. The flysheet was hooked up between the top of the wardrobe and the window, while two damp cycling shirts were on hangers suspended out of it. Battery chargers and a camera fought for space on the table with Michelin maps, green guides and the book I was reading. My notebook and a few postcards were on the floor by the bed, and my shoes and helmet (containing sweaty gloves and bandana) were where I'd left them, just inside the door. A couple of carrier-bags dividing clean clothes from dirty ones sat on the chair.

This might just sound like mess, but there was a great sense of achievement to be gained from forcing it all back into the panniers in a set pattern. Like a Buddhist meditation, I can still picture all the items going into each bag in order, and the number of times I'd have to roll over the tops – the warmer the day, the fewer rolls, as the waterproof and fleece were packed away. After a quick idiot check, I was downstairs. The waitress from the night before was serving breakfast (and had probably been down to buy the bread too) in tracksuit bottoms and a T-shirt, with her hair down. So, this was what she looked like the next morning: good. As I was checking out, she asked me about my final destination.

'*La Suisse et l'Italie, en vélo?*'

'*Oui,*' I said, all casual.

She looked up from the cash register, and fixed me with an earnest gaze. '*Bon courage, Monsieur,*' she said.

I blushed. *Bon courage?* How cool. How French. I felt like I was heading off to fight for a noble cause. A musketeer on a bike. Who couldn't talk to women, even when it was clear they liked me.

8

Melting Roads and Dirty Showers

Ater a week of wide-open spaces, I wasn't looking forward to jousting with the traffic on the way into Nantes. But early on the roads were still empty, and as I rode past one shady house, the warm air carried to me the sound of someone playing the piano inside. This small and lovely moment sounds like a cheesy advertisement by the French tourist authority, but it happened.

The traffic increased as I approached the city, but bicycle paths appeared and led me away from the dual carriageways and tricky junctions. Getting closer to the centre of town, the cars disappeared, and I was sharing the road with trains from the light rail network.

I'd imagined Nantes to be a dull industrial sprawl, but the spacious city centre boasts broad avenues, a lofty cathedral and an impressive château. I dumped the bike and enjoyed an urbane lunch at a café in one of the large squares.

Nantes is an important place in the Columbanus story, but it also shows the frustrations inherent in following his journeys because he was probably here twice. The first time was when he'd just arrived in France and, having spent some time in Brittany, set out further east. At that time Brittany was overrun by Celtic religious men, who gave their names to places that survive today. St Malo and St Cadoc were Welsh, and they were joined by many refugees from Britain, fleeing both plague and the Anglo-Saxon invaders. Brittany's Celtic roots were still showing – it had never been fully settled by the Romans, and during Columbanus's time, the Frankish kings' writ scarcely ran west of the river Vilaine. In fact, there were so many Britons arriving to seek refuge with their Celtic cousins that the area became known as Lesser Britain (and, from that, Brittany). As a result, Britain started to be called 'Great Britain' to distinguish it from this piece of France, not because there was anything particularly great about it.

So, as foreign locations went, Brittany wouldn't have felt unfamiliar to Columbanus, and the connections between Ireland and Brittany are still clear today. Many places are twinned with Irish towns, and road signs are in both French and Breton, a Celtic language similar to Irish and Welsh. Maybe the area felt too similar to Columbanus: his biographer Jonas says that the monk and his party 'discussed their plans anxiously, until finally they decided to enter the land of Gaul'. And it was probably during his journey inland that he came through Nantes, a city of some prominence.

As we've seen, towns of any sort would have been a new concept to the Irishmen, and here was one of the long-standing administrative and trading centres of the Roman Empire. Even under the control of Frankish invaders, cities in Gaul retained much of their importance, and the new kings were careful to adopt Roman customs and support the Gallo-Roman administrators and bishops who kept things working. The company had been sold to new owners from overseas, but civil society continued much as before.

The stone buildings, statues, cobbled roads and bustle of people spending money would have underlined to Columbanus that he was far from home on his first visit to the city. Many years later, in 610, he was expelled from his monasteries in eastern France and escorted across the country and back to Nantes, to be put on a merchant ship for Ireland. While he was waiting by the harbour, he took the opportunity to write one last letter to his followers who remained in Luxeuil; the text survives today. From it we get a clear image of a deeply saddened man. He gives advice to the monk Attala, who is to take his place as abbot, and asks him to give to another monk 'my kiss, which then in his hurry, he did not receive'. He comments, 'I wanted to write you a tearful letter', but he restrains himself, 'so my speech has been outwardly made smooth, and grief is shut up within'. In some ways that's true: the letter is written in Columbanus's customary precise and lucid Latin, but besides the exhortations to obedience and humility, there are clear signs of his grief at the disputes that have forced him to leave his home of twenty years: 'I confess that I am broken on this account – while I wished to help all those who fought against me without cause when I spoke to them, and while I trusted all, I have been almost driven mad.' You can almost see him struggling to contain his emotions while he waits for the boat. At one point, he apologises for the rambling nature of the letter – 'love does not keep order, so my missive is confused' – and, with a startling immediacy across nearly 1400 years, he tells us: 'Now, as I write, a messenger has reached me, saying that the ship is ready for me, in which I shall be carried unwittingly to my country.'

I rode a little out of the centre of Nantes to get my first

glimpse of the Loire, where Columbanus's boat would have been waiting. The river is broad and powerful here, and Columbanus ordered his belongings to be put aboard the ship. He was going to journey out to the mouth of the river in a skiff, to board the ship there. But, according to Jonas, as the ship headed out to the ocean with a favourable wind, 'a huge wave came and drove the vessel on shore. It stuck fast on the land and, with the water receding, remained quietly in the channel. The bark remained high and dry for three days.' At this point, the captain recognised a miracle in progress, and took Columbanus's belongings off the ship. His companions disembarked and everyone agreed that God did not want Columbanus to return home. Interestingly, however, Columbanus's letter (written before the boat sailed, remember) includes the line, 'If I escape there is no guard to prevent it, for they seem to desire it,' suggesting that perhaps the miracle was a later cover for what was simply his stubbornness. Either way, the saint and his followers turned back inland and began the journey that would eventually take them to Switzerland.

So you have Columbanus in Nantes twice. Ironically, we have most of the information about the journey the wrong way round: Jonas recounts all the towns the disappointed monks travelled through on their way there. This meant that as I was travelling down the Loire, I'd have met Columbanus coming back the other way.

Just behind the elegant roofed shopping arcade in the centre of town, I found an Internet café to check my email and update my website. As a recovering dot-commer, I had my own site. I'd fallen into technology work, and thought I'd leave within six months. Sitting in a cube farm in

Clonskeagh all day was miserable – the only relief was the tea-breaks when you could talk to all the other tech writers in the company. Everyone had a half-finished novel in their desk drawer, or a colourful history of freelance work. Nobody wanted to be doing this, but the pay was OK and we could moan about the editors, as if we were writing things we cared about. Our days were the same colour as our computers – not quite grey and not quite beige. Greige.

It was a form of digital factory labour, but there was an opportunity to play with the new-fangled Internet, and I became interested in the technology I was writing about. I finally escaped from the grind to become employee number eight at Ireland's most famous and most chaotic website developers. There was a maverick spirit to the place, where a team of talented if wayward souls were making things up as they went along. Our big-name clients knew less than we did, and bought into the outrageous claims of our guru-style boss. 'We're digging in the digital soil, lads,' he said. Of course we were. Not only that, we offered 'New Thinking for the Digital Age' – it said so on our business cards.

Success brought structures and schedules, and when the days threatened to turn greige again, I jumped ship and ended up in Kansas, working as our man on the prairies for another tech company. I helped lecturers at Kansas State University prepare their teaching materials to be turned into online training by the folks back in Dublin, and as long as the supply of material kept coming, I was left on my own. Having a boss several thousand miles away was a great improvement, especially as the time difference meant that no one would be calling after midday, because in Ireland they'd all have gone home. I wasn't that busy, and it was great to be back in a college environment, with the president of the university inviting me to lunch to talk about the fall of the Roman Empire. But it was in Kansas, where being liberal meant using a lot of bullets to shoot at the road signs, and after a time I wanted to move on.

I didn't fancy a return to Dublin, so I was transferred to the Silicon Valley, the centre of the high-tech explosion. Many people there thought they were changing the world, and that they would make their fortunes doing it, but I just wanted to live in San Francisco – the exact opposite of Kansas. The flaw in my brilliant plan was that I'd taken the job for the food, culture and outdoor opportunities, but now they wanted me to go to work. I always felt I was playing a role and would be found out sooner or later. My job title said I was principal research editor, but I didn't even know what that meant.

At least I was working for an Irish company, so there were still some flashes of humour amid the frightening earnestness of those who saw themselves as the architects of a new age. One day in a meeting with a partner company we went round the table doing introductions. Patrick and I were both from the other side of the water, our visitors were all locals.

'Why don't we explain our roles, and then say something about ourselves, just to break the ice a little?' one suggested. 'I'll start,' he continued. 'I'm Mike, and I'm the e-marketing director on the project. I've been with the company a year, and I coach a Little League team on the weekends.'

'Great. And I'm Hank – Mike's assistant. I graduated first in my biz-school class at Duke, and I've just moved out here. I live in the Marina district in the city.'

'My name's Barbara?' said Barbara, her voice going up at

the end as if she wasn't quite sure. 'I'll be the design lead? And my daughter's on the honour roll at her school?'

Now it was my turn. I went for the conservative option: 'I'm David, I'll be editing and approving the content of this. When I get time, I like to ride bikes.'

Then Patrick looked up and said, 'I'm Paddy, the project manager. I once broke both my arms jumping off the roof of a building.'

There was a silence as people tried to work out if he was joking. They hadn't really decided when he continued, 'Of course, I was completely pissed at the time.'

Apart from moments like that, the work was very demanding – I took an average of one flight a week during those three years in the States, and I seldom saw my apartment in daylight. Only the outrageous pay cheques helped. In the end, although my boss warned me that if I left I'd never be rich, I decided to cut and run. I still feel like there's unfinished business for me in the States, but I returned home because I wanted my life back.

But old tech habits die hard, and before I set out on the bike trip I'd built a website describing my adventure, and now, as I sat in Nantes, I wrote a brief report on the story so far. It had to be brief because my typing wasn't going well. Who knew French computer keyboards were laid out differently? Instead of the familiar QWERTY layout, they are AZERT – zhqt zqs I to do?

I soon rejoined my bike and my current occupation: hot-weather cyclist. I felt I was pretending at this too, but I was in the middle of it now, so I had to keep going. I followed one of the light rail lines out of the city, stopped for more water and suntan lotion on the edge of town, then met up with the

Loire again. It's so wide that the first bridge I rode over came in two parts. The first span crossed to a sandy island in the middle of the river and the second deposited me on the south bank. In the afternoon heat I followed the road through villages that seemed to turn their backs on the river, nestling down a little from the road built along the embankment. The sightlines were long and open, and whitewashed red-tiled houses had replaced the Breton brown-stone buildings.

I was counting on the road being flat alongside the river, especially in this harsh weather. For the first fifteen kilometres after the bridge I sped along, creating my own breeze, which made it cooler to be cycling than to be stopped. But as I reached the last half-hour of the day's ride, the road veered away from the river and headed up a sharp climb. I was out of the saddle as I leant forward and muscled the front of the bike from side to side. Cyclists have a suitably Anglo-Saxon word for this: they call it 'honking', and the sun pushed down on my shoulders as I honked through the heavy air, my pulse pounding in my head.

Then it was downhill again to the campsite near the river, where a friendly woman had me fill in a long registration form while I dripped sweat on to her table. It was as if a suitable degree of bureaucracy was required to cover the fact that you were paying almost nothing to sleep in someone's field. I felt dizzy while I was putting my tent up in my hedge-bound rectangle so I ate a lot of dried apricots and watched ants crawl around the outside of my panniers. Cycling in hot weather had taken its toll.

In the early evening I walked up the steep hill and back to the village. I was dripping with sweat by the time I got there and discovered that the bar was closed. There was no one around, and I walked further along the road with a growing sense that my stomach was churning. As I reached a roadside bar with a couple of cars parked outside, I suddenly felt very cold. Inside the bar the television was talking to itself, but a rotund landlady appeared and ushered me into the empty dining room. I wasn't sure food was such a good idea, especially as I was the only person in the place, but I sat down long enough to see that there wasn't a menu, then got up again and walked briskly to the bathroom. This condition was a sudden and unpleasant surprise, but I didn't feel any nausea or pain, so maybe food and drink would be a help.

Back at my table there was still no menu, but a carafe of red wine had appeared, and the landlady gestured towards the chilled cabinet in the corner. This had been covered and switched off when I'd first sat down, but now it had hummed into life, and contained terrines of pâté, tuna fish and cold meat, along with bowls of salad. There was a grey hue to a lot of the substances, which had clearly been there since lunchtime, but I didn't seem to have many other options. Was this all there was to eat? The landlady had disappeared again, so I piled my plate high, utilising structural techniques learnt at the Pizza Hut salad bar during teenage birthday parties. I wondered if I'd been struck down with a form of heat exhaustion, or fast-acting food poisoning from the apricots. In my current state, the hors d'oeuvres would be a type of Loire roulette, but I didn't seem to be getting any worse. In fact, my mood was improving with the red wine. The landlady reappeared to ask if I'd like beef or ham – so there was at least one more course. Stray kids were wandering around in the bar, and this certainly wasn't the sort of place you'd find in a guidebook. Based on the lack of customers, it didn't look like you'd find it in the phonebook either.

The gammon steak was very salty, and I turned down the offer of desserts from the top of the unchilled chilled cabinet, but I was so delighted I could walk out of the place in reasonable shape that I really didn't mind. Outside, the sun was setting over the valley, making a golden ribbon of the river and creating avenues of shadow as it caught the tops of the vines. Not a bad place to have a mystery stomach ailment. I walked past the old church and found my way back to the campsite along footpaths through vineyards. It was still humid, and for the first time I was in a landscape that couldn't be found in Ireland. Columbanus would definitely have felt a stranger here.

Lying in the tent I could see the stars through the open flysheet doors. I sweated gently on top of my sleeping-bag, taunting the mosquitoes buzzing outside.

The next afternoon it was so hot that bits of the road were melting. First I noticed a quiet, regular click, which came from a piece of gravel in the front tyre. Normally, they are just wedged into the tread, but this time it was stuck on with tar. Curious. I removed it, and started off again. I'd not gone far when I noticed a similar sound coming from the back tyre. The same problem. This time I'd stopped where two slabs of smooth black Euromacadam joined, and as I poked my shoe into the tar used to seal the join, it squidged like freshly chewed gum. The temperature gauge on my watch said it was 37 degrees Celsius – hot enough to melt roads.

The village of Béhuard offered some shade and a

fifteenth-century church built on a rock. The village sits on a spit of land in the middle of the river, with the church at the end. It had been built by Louis XI on the site of a fifth-century oratory to commemorate his salvation from drowning in a shipwreck. The rock rises to the height of a house above the rest of the island, and it juts into the church, creating a cave-like interior. A balcony is suspended over the nave, and a large golden crucifix hangs over the altar. I took a seat near the aisle and watched a swallow swooping around the balcony, trilling happily as it went. During my Silicon Valley travelling days, I always felt as if I was waiting for my soul to catch up. Once I'd been in Cincinnati airport waiting for a plane, and half a dozen birds were flying around inside the terminal building. They perched on the tall trees in pots near the Starbucks, and zoomed across the glass enclosure laughing at the wingless humans who had to get into big metal tubes to fly.

I'd left the bike outside in the sun and the display on my trip computer had died with the heat. It wasn't far now to Angers, and with nothing else on the road (mad dogs and Englishmen and all that), I went over a few sharp climbs amid the vineyards before I reached the outskirts of town. The interface between the big yellow Michelin maps and the town plans in the guidebooks wasn't always perfect, and it took a while to find the centre of town, with its deep-moated castle and huge round towers. After the previous night's down-home meal and sweltering tent I was due some luxury, and the helpful folks in the nicely air-conditioned tourist office booked me a room in a pricy hotel.

'Hotel Ibis?' the woman at the tourist office had asked, her tone suggesting it was a duff choice but because I was

English she couldn't be bothered to explain why. She was right. I'd been looking for historic understated charm; instead I got business-traveller anonymous efficiency. Later I ran into this chain of hotels all over the country, but I'd had no idea I was booking into a place with piped music and a whiteboard in Reception for conference delegates' messages. Encouragingly, one of the corporate seminar rooms had been turned into a bike park for the summer, and a selection of tourers, racers and solid German hybrid bikes was already lined up waiting for the presentation on this year's sales targets.

My room's biggest strength was its bath, so the bike kit and I had a soak before I headed back into the mad heat to explore the castle and the cathedral. I really wanted to laze around for a while, but I was leaving early the next morning so had only a few hours to get a feel of the place before food and sleep beckoned. I snuck into the château half an hour before it closed, and clambered around the battlements and towers before I was brought up short in front of the fourteenth-century Tapestry of the Apocalypse. Around 350 feet in length, the tapestry stretches around three walls of a climate-controlled bunker underneath the castle. The doors have an airlock system with a filter to remove dust from your clothes before you walk in – very *Star Trek*. In fact, the tapestry reads like a *Star Trek* episode on an epic scale. The evil dragon is shown big and nasty in lots of frames, like the alien life-form that threatens the *Enterprise*. Two-thirds of the way through, the Beast is getting all the adoration, lots of people with non-speaking parts have been killed, and you can't see how the Lamb's going to get out of this one. But it's all sorted out in the last few frames, the good guys win and

Captain Kirk gets to say, 'On Earth, we call this kissing.' The 'sing a new song' image is wonderful, and the new Jerusalem looks a lot like Angers must have when the tapestry was made.

Early next morning was beautiful as I rode alongside the glassy Loire. Further downstream there had been as much sand as water in the river, and campsites used the dried-up banks as beaches. Here the river had more enthusiasm, and with the hazy sun still low in the sky, anglers were out in boats and the villages had a lazy Saturday-morning feel. The miles just appeared under the wheels and I munched happily on a *pain au chocolat*.

The village of Cunault boasted a Romanesque church of rare white elegance. The sun shone in the rounded arch windows, illuminating the soaring space. I took the same photograph I'd tried in every church I'd entered – stand at the back, turn the camera on its side and try to capture the sweep of the view up the aisle to the altar. Looking at the pictures later, it was hard to tell one gorgeous bit of vaulting from another, but at least I'd tried. When I'm at home, I hardly ever enter a church, but here I was dashing into chapels, cathedrals and oratories like a candle delivery-man. I'd always rationalised the attraction as historical and architectural, but I couldn't deny the sense of calm and reflection I often came away with.

In the afternoon, I had an appointment with my high-school medieval-history class. Since arriving at the Loire, I'd felt I was back in the classroom while my teacher led us through Angevins, Plantagenets and the machinations of other men in armour. The maps were full of places I half

remembered, and I struggled to separate historical recoll-
ections from stray bits of information about Elvis Costello,
Greta Scacchi, Arsenal Football Club and other sixth-form
preoccupations. But I was about to hit the motherlode of
medieval history in the area: Fontevraud Abbey, last resting-
place of English monarchs Henry II and his son Richard the
Lionheart.

I missed the entrance to the abbey and found another hill
to climb before I arrived, leaving the bike in the shade, its
sweaty flanks heaving. The main chapel in the complex is
built of the same nearly white stone as Cunault, and there in
the long nave stood the royal tombs. The redoubtable
Eleanor of Aquitaine lay beside her husband Henry II, while
Richard the Lionheart was next to his sister-in-law, Isabella
of Angoulême.

From Napoleonic times until the 1960s the abbey was
a prison, and the fabric of the buildings was severely
damaged. After most of the inmates had left, a few remained
with orders to restore the place before the first visitors
arrived. There are any number of cloistered courtyards,
vaulted refectories and even a rare octagonal cookhouse. It
was busy with tourists kicking up white dust as they walked
from building to building, and there was still restoration
work going on, but it was more than worth the effort it had
taken to get there.

It was just a few downhill minutes back to the river and
the three-star campsite at the village of Montsoreau, which
had a facility that suddenly seemed very attractive. I jumped
into the swimming-pool still wearing my cycling shorts,
scaring the English kids getting sunburnt in the shallow end.
Then it was time for a quick shower. The bathrooms were

three-star clean, and I was enjoying the warm water cascading over me when I heard a noise in the cubicle next to me. I thought it was a suppressed laugh, then sensed some kind of breathlessly exerted silence. Then a slim bronzed hand appeared below the divider, palm down on the floor. While I was trying to work out the gymnastic ramifications of this manoeuvre, there was a muffled bump as another bit of body hit the cubicle wall. It went breathlessly quiet for a time and the hand disappeared. In my imagined version of this encounter, the door to my cubicle opened, and the glistening girl invited herself in. Of course, in the world of embarrassed diffidence I inhabited, I hurriedly left the couple to it, trying to be as quiet as I could so as not to disturb them. They were having sex in the shower, and I was the one blushing. Sometimes an English upbringing is too much to bear.

The walk to dinner took my mind off it. The view towards the river included the graceful mass of Montsoreau's château in the foreground, and a hot-air balloon rising in the distance. The whole scene was bathed in a warm light, and upstream you could see the fork in the river where the Vienne entered the Loire. I lucked into a free table on a busy Saturday night at the best restaurant in the village. A half-bottle of wine from Saumur arrived with the outside of its ice bucket frosted with condensation, and good food followed. I looked around. None of the diners seemed to have come from the campsite. Maybe there was an un-written rule that sleeping under canvas meant you had to eat underdone pasta cooked over a sputtering stove. Well, not this camping renegade. Where's the dessert menu?

9

Any Tent in a Storm

On a rainy morning in Cambridge in the autumn of 1990, the cold wind was blowing unobstructed from the North Sea, and all the other arts undergraduates were tucked up in bed. Unfortunately, students of Anglo-Saxon, Norse and Celtic had lectures scheduled for nine a.m. – like the scientists, if you can believe it – and the department was so small that attendance was all but mandatory. On the first day of our first term, we'd been told that while English students and historians might choose to involve themselves in extra-curricular activities such as sport, drama, eating or sleeping, we, as the stormtroopers of Dark Age studies, should under no circumstances countenance such distractions.

So I stumbled down the stairs from my room and headed out through the back gate of college for the walk to the department off West Road. Today's lecture was part of the History of the Celtic-Speaking Peoples paper, and concerned early Irish monasticism. Our wild-haired lecturer was de-bunking the myth that the Irish had saved civilisation by hoarding classical manuscripts while the rest of Europe was in turmoil. The truth was that monks were well versed in the subjects that interested them – grammar, astronomy, biblical exegesis – but had no knowledge of Virgil, Horace and the like.

The second part of the myth was that these Irish scholars then fanned out across the Continent, bringing learning to the benighted barbarians who had overthrown the Roman Empire. Again, this was only adjacent to the truth at best: there was more continuity during the Dark Ages than had earlier been thought and we owe a greater debt to the Moors than to the Irish for the preservation and transmission of classical texts. What a let-down. I'd got out of bed to be told that a cool story wasn't really that cool after all. But just as we were approaching the end of the hour, the lecturer said, 'Well, of course, there's one exception to that rule. Columbanus. He's something of an exception to every rule.'

I looked up. Who?

'Columbanus was perhaps the earliest and best-travelled of the Irish monks who crossed to Europe. He founded monasteries in what are now France, Austria and Italy, he brought the Irish practice of private penance and confession to Europe, and his followers were responsible for founding over a hundred monasteries within a century of his death around 615.'

That sounded more like it: a local boy made good. I hit the books and discovered that, unlike most figures from that period, it was possible to establish something of his character, behind the miracles and the fulsome praise for his piety. The reason for his success became clear: he was a monster. The rules he wrote for his monasteries show his attitudes clearly. As one historian pointed out, 'For Columbanus the flesh is "unclean by nature", the body a prison, and the monk must fight in Christ's host against the vices which constantly assail him.'

But it was hard not to be impressed by his achievements.

I thought of the man from Carlow crossing the Alps, writing to Pope Gregory the Great in ornate Latin, and seeking solitude in an Apennine valley. He was not only the first Irish man of letters, he was the first certified Irish expat, thinking fondly of home as he went abroad to do great things. His was a story of writing, stubbornness and exile – what's more Irish than that?

Later, Columbanus got lost again amid the rest of my studies – Old Irish grammar, medieval Latin neologisms and witness lists from Anglo-Saxon writs. But I remembered him as a man who stood out amid the ranks of shadowy figures that inhabit early medieval studies.

I'd been neglecting Columbanus since I left Nantes. But now I could correct that, as the area around Tours was home to one of his heroes – St Martin, perhaps the most prominent saint of the early medieval period. I woke up early on Sunday morning and stole out of the campsite quietly. Just down the road was Candes St Martin, a small village with a church dedicated to the saint, who was born around 316 in what is now Hungary. He served as a Roman legionary in France, and one day in Amiens he was approached by a beggar dressed in rags. Our hero took his sword, cut his cloak in two and gave half to the beggar. Later, Jesus came to him in a dream, wearing the tattered cloak. A convert to the new religion of Christianity, Martin became a monk, then Bishop of Tours, but continued to live as a monk and founded a monastery at nearby Marmoutiers. His piety and devotion were renowned far and wide, helped by the influential *Life* written by Sulpicius Severus, and his starring role in Gregory of Tours' *History of the Franks*.

He is buried in his basilica in Tours, but he died

downstream at Candes, and was first interred there. Such was its prestige that his body was all but stolen by his monks, and carried back up the river overnight. But the Romanesque church at Candes still has a beautifully carved porch and a fine location. I scampered up the hill behind it to get a view of the Vienne meeting the Loire, then descended to follow the Vienne to Chinon – yet another in the succession of medieval riverside towns with a historic château and narrow, cobbled streets.

There, a *café au lait* reminded me I hadn't been stopping often enough for coffee. Every morning after a night of camping I always meant to pause after a brief spell of cycling for some caffeine, but it never happened. Cyclists have a particular fondness for cake and coffee. Perhaps it was the temperature – I was always keen to get more kilometres done before the roads were melting. Today I was heading to Tours, but there were any number of fairytale châteaux on the way and the first I came to when I rejoined the Loire was at Ussé.

I like my castles windswept and rugged, or at least practical, and Ussé let me down. Any castle that couldn't be defended against the military technology of the time in which it was built seems like a con to me – a big house with pretty turrets isn't a castle, it's just a big house with turrets. But it does look amazing – as the many visitors taking pictures obviously recognised. A quiet road directly alongside the Loire took me to the next fake castle, and I passed more touring cyclists in a ninety-minute stretch than I'd seen in the previous week.

After my picnic lunch in some welcome shade at Villandry I joined the queues on their way into the next château. It was lovely in a rococo way, but I spent most of my time inside looking out of the windows at the breath-taking formal gardens. Perhaps a dozen stretched out into the distance, with several lakes, sundry arbours and shady avenues, a herb garden and a manicured 'wilderness' area. Every detail was perfect and the scale was spectacular. In the more exposed places on my walk round, I ran into coach parties' elderly stragglers, left for the vultures on the raked and baking gravel. It was foolishly hot, and having been tempted outside by the lure of expert gardening, these poor souls didn't have the strength to make it back into the shade – forget Inigo Jones, you needed Indiana under these conditions.

It was sixteen kilometres to Tours, and I drained my water-bottles and made a dash for the city. I got a room on the top floor of a small hotel, and from the open window I could see across the rooftops to St Martin's on my left and the cathedral on my right. I sat down on the bed and worked out that I had come 526 kilometres since my last day off in Cancale. That made it 971 kilometres since Dublin, which sounded an impressively large number.

The big distances had come as a side-effect of focusing on a small stretch at any one time, and here I was helped by the makers of my handlebar-bag. Before setting off each day, I'd fold the appropriate map into a contorted shape in the map case so that just the part I needed for the morning's ride was visible. I'd stop and display the next few kilometres as necessary. In this way I'd inched my way across the whole of map *230*, *Bretagne*, and was now in the middle folds of *232*, *Pays de Loire*. A project management expert I know avoids drift on a long job by arranging 'inch pebbles' between the milestones. My inch pebbles were the ends of what could be displayed in the map case at any one time. As long as you were heading in the right direction, there was no point in worrying about anything else beyond the most immediate terrain. I should have left it at that, but instead I unfolded the maps and looked at longer distances and cities that were far away. Until now the plan for the trip had been simple – ride from the ferry to the place where Columbanus landed, then down to Nantes and along the Loire. But in a few days I'd have to leave the river behind as it turned south after Orléans. On the maps I caught glimpses of mountains off to the east; I was perhaps only a third of the way to Bobbio, and the easiest third at that. I got a little wobbly imagining ugly slogs and unfriendly people in eastern France and Switzerland. Time to put away the maps and get something to eat.

I wasn't helped by the bustle and energy of Tours on a summer Sunday night. Tourists mingled with students and dogs on strings in a setting of *faux*-Irish bars and kebab shops. It was just like Dublin. After a day of pastoral scenes and elegant châteaux, I wasn't able for this. I found my way to a busy Italian restaurant and was seated just inside the door so I could be bumped by everyone coming in and out, and had an excellent view of the stress-fuelled kitchen. Looking for peace and urbane service I found chaos and sweaty tension. I beat a hasty retreat to my room.

When Columbanus had stopped in Tours on his way back to Nantes, he had carried out an overnight vigil at the tomb of St Martin. The church that he knew is now long gone, although two towers from a later medieval version remain, divided by more recent streets. The current basilica of St

Martin has a different alignment from the older versions, but the tomb of the saint in the crypt is in much the same position as it would have been in Columbanus's time. So, Monday morning saw me walking down the stairs into the crypt.

It's a large space, with the tomb at the far end. Columbanus had been here, on this exact spot, paying his respects to St Martin with an overnight vigil. Prayers and dedications from people who wanted to be remembered were painted on many of the stones of the vaulted ceiling. I knelt before the tomb as Columbanus had. With my hands clasped in front of me, I found myself asking for blessings from St Martin. Suddenly tears welled in my eyes and dropped on to the floor beside the tomb. After a time, I got up, lit a candle, then went to sit down and compose myself. Columbanus would have had little time for such a display of weakness, but I felt closer to him here than ever before. He was severe and uncompromising, but these seemed like admirable qualities. The only thing I was certain about was my uncertainty about everything. I envied him his vocation and clarity. Maybe if I followed him all the way to Italy, some of his bloody-mindedness would rub off on me.

But even when you've had a deeply emotional moment at ten thirty on a Monday morning, you've still got the rest of the day to fill. Across the river at the edge of town, the site of St Martin's abbey at Marmoutier was a disappointment. Monks had carved cells into the walls of the cliff above the river, and some were still visible, but the abbey itself (in a much later incarnation) is now a private school with private grounds, so I'd schlepped a long way for little profit. That evening, the most exciting part of my meal came from sitting outside a restaurant across the road from a video shop. The whole of the shopfront was taken up by a video screen, keypad and a couple of metal letterboxes. It looked like an ATM on steroids, and it allowed punters to choose a movie from the computer display, swipe their cashpoint card, then walk away with the videotape. This appealed to the geek in me, especially as all French shops seemed to be closed much more than they were open.

Tuesday morning saw me back on the bike, riding eastwards for more château action. Amboise castle had a medieval look to it, but the souvenir shops and tourists put me off. I left the Loire for a time, and dropped down to Chenonceau, where another stately pile awaited me. It had a grace and coherence that some of the other places lacked, and the glorious gallery that stretched across the river made the queuing to get into every room bearable.

I'd half intended to camp that night, after my two days' hotelling in Tours, but there was no campsite as I approached Blois so I found my way to the Grand Hôtel de France. There's a thin line between attractively faded elegance and just plain tatty, but this place was so far over into the tat column that it wasn't funny. The proprietress seemed unhappy at having been disturbed by a paying customer, and booked me into a dog-eared room that looked out on to a brick wall. But at least the hotel was close to the château, a mad amalgam of different architectural styles and periods of construction. As with Angers, visiting in the last hour of the day gave me peace and quiet I'd not had all day, and the only crowd I found came at the end of my tour. In a lofty hall, a trio was playing Mozart to an attentive audience.

Another night in a hotel had set me thinking about how

much money I was spending. The fact that everything had been going so well was a worry, and in lieu of any real problems I made myself anxious about expenditure. This was easily done as I had no idea how much I'd spent – some larger bills went on the credit card and I got cash from ATMs for everything else. Most things were cheap by Dublin standards, especially accommodation and food (my major expenses), and I was nowhere near the loose daily allowance I'd set for myself. But I wasn't going to let the facts get in the way of a quick panic, so as I sat down at a restaurant that evening I chose the cheapest menu they had. I got what I deserved: the main course was a slab of stringy grey meat so tough the table swayed vigorously when I tried to cut it. I couldn't identify it, let alone eat it. I admitted defeat.

Things seemed out of joint that evening, so I returned to my threadbare room and went for an early night. In the morning, the grumpy proprietress was showing little sympathy for a Dutch couple whose car had been broken into outside the hotel. She further proved her lack of suitability for a job in the hospitality industry by insisting that she couldn't take credit cards for bills of less than three hundred francs, and charging me ten francs for letting me park my bike in the garage.

I was pleased to leave her behind and aim for Chambord, my last Loire château. It was an epic of a house, with huge rooms, an estate stretching away to the horizon and a double spiral staircase that purported to have been designed by Leonardo da Vinci, who spent some time in the area at the behest of François I. Even the roof was spectacular, with any number of spires and glass towers creating a fantastical crystal forest on high. The place was on such a scale that it absorbed any number of tourists without complaint. The next stop was Orléans, where I'd planned to finish the day's ride after another seventy hot kilometres. Joan of Arc's city offered wide boulevards but it didn't grab me. The nearest campsite was over thirty kilometres further upstream, and as I rode out of the city I repeated, 'Velvet,' to myself. Ride like velvet, all soft and smooth.

The kilometres came easily, and I was singing to myself when I was stung again. You wait thirty years for one sting, and then … I felt the insect fly down the neck of my jersey, put my hand to my left ribs, and experienced a sharp puncture. I stopped and pulled up my jersey to let the creature escape, then performed the same first-aid routine I'd adopted in Wicklow. With the singing I was lucky the bee hadn't flown into my mouth.

I reached the small village of Germigny-des-Prés, which has the most beautiful Carolingian church I've ever seen. Built around 800, it has a simple grace that made me grin after the flamboyance of the châteaux. There were no other tourists, and I walked around its warm ochre exterior before heading inside to look at the glorious mosaic in the apse. The whitewash, wooden beams and simple layout spoke of a devotion that was both humble and strong. I'd seen soaring Gothic cathedrals, Renaissance palaces and baroque flights of fancy, but this squat village church beat them all.

The hundred-kilometre mark for the day came up just before I arrived at the campsite beside the river at Benoît-sur-Loire. After dinner in the only restaurant in town, I rode back along the path that ran from the town to the campsite and saw dark clouds gathering off to the west.

The rain started to come down just as I'd zipped myself into the tent.

Soon thunder and lightning filled the sky and it sounded as if the tent was being pebble-dashed. I wasn't sure how it would cope with the deluge. After about an hour of buffeting, I carefully checked the inner tent for water; nothing had got through the flysheet from above. But then I shifted my weight near the door of the tent and felt a pool of water through the fabric of the tent under my hand. The ground was sandy and the water had run off the fly and found its way into a hollow below me. I wasn't hopeful that the lightweight layers of nylon would be enough to keep out the water for long, so I did a Walter Raleigh impression with my waterproof jacket, laying it across the puddle. It was hard to avoid sleeping on the wet patch, as I could scarcely move without pressing the side of the tent against the soaked flysheet, so I checked and checked again, but no water came up from beneath or in from above. Eventually the rain eased, and the pool under the tent disappeared as I dozed off, scoring that bout to the feisty yellow featherweight.

It was my last day on the Loire, and since Blois the towns had looked ordinary after the flat-out loveliness of the earlier ones. I grabbed a coffee in Sully, which had a medieval castle but didn't seem inclined to make a fuss about it. Outside a baker's I met a heavy, middle-aged Belgian cyclist with a big beard and a bigger set of bags on his groaning mountain bike. He was riding to South Africa, sleeping in barns and anywhere else he could find.

'I just stop and ask someone when I don't want to go any further for the day. People are very kind,' he said.

'When do you think you'll make it to South Africa?'

'I don't have a watch, and I don't really do time,' he said. 'Perhaps next year, but I've got the rest of my life.'

Fair enough. He seemed a little mad, but I guess to an outside observer there was almost no difference between us – the Lycra clothes, the laden bikes, the cyclist's tan – even the great distances we planned to cover. His life must have broken in some way to prompt this mad journey – who can just pack up and head across a continent or two? Who would want to? Had my life broken too?

But if we were similar in some ways, there were differences too. He'd been talking to people, sleeping in their barns, relying on the comfort of strangers. I'd been relying on the elasticity of my credit card. I had enough French to order dinner and get a hotel room, but I'd hardly spoken to anyone. I was on a mobile retreat, and if I was auditioning for the new role of travel writer, wasn't I supposed to give prose portraits of the characters I met, and rough it a little for the sake of adventure? It had bucketed with rain last night and I hadn't even got wet. Things were going too well. What was I going to write about?

10

Serendipity and Soccer

If they kicked that door any harder it was going to fly off its hinges. They generated some power from the kick itself, but most of it came from the speed of their approach. The husband went for the straight frontward boot, while his wife performed a 180-degree spin just as she got to the door, followed by a mule-like backwards jab with her heel. She then rolled round the opening door, perfectly balancing the tray as she disappeared into the kitchen.

Another restaurant in a small country hotel, and I was watching my hosts rush around as if they were training for events at the gastronomic Olympics. They were frighteningly efficient but also a little disconcerting, as there were only four people eating in the whole place. Discounting the drama of their waiting style, the food was great. Commitment to the quality of food even in the smallest French town was amazing. Dublin was congratulating itself on its newfound foodieness, and ham and cheese toasties were now called prosciutto and mozzarella panini, but we were a long way from this.

I'd arrived outside a bar in Bléneau in the middle of the afternoon, unsure if I was going to go any further that day. The owner appeared and started putting out the chairs and tables again after the threat of rain had passed. She asked me if I was looking for a place to stay. That made up my mind for me, and soon I was installed in a large, old-fashioned room above the bar, with flowers in the window-box and enough room to hang up my damp tent and still move around. I'd showered and was slathering my long-suffering backside with soothing Sudocrem when I heard a key turning in the lock of the door. Time moved slowly as the door opened and an unsuspecting teenage girl walked in carrying an armful of towels. There wasn't much else I could do, so I smiled and tried a cheery '*Bonjour*', while showing her my bare essentials. Before I'd finished the second syllable, she'd gasped, apologised and fled the room. There were two possible outcomes from this situation. Either her father would soon appear and start talking to me about a dowry, or a posse would arrive to drum me out of town. 'How dare you show your ugly white backside to one of our daughters? You English dog!' When it was time for dinner, I crept downstairs and hoped I wouldn't run into her again.

The pace of a day's cycling lent serendipity to the places I ended up. I'd now turned away from the Loire, and it was great to be in Bléneau because there was no reason for a tourist to be there. I was only there because it was a convenient distance from yesterday's storm-tossed campsite and tomorrow's date with the Roman city of Auxerre. If you were travelling by car, you'd be on the main roads so you'd never even go through it on your way somewhere else.

The kitchen door swung wildly again, and the hostess arrived, breathless, with my dessert. If your only complaint about your meal is the gung-ho fashion in which it's brought to you, things can't be all bad.

I was on to another map the next morning (*238, Centre Berry-Nivernais*), and into a different sort of cycling. An hour out of Bléneau I was beginning to see what happened when you left the river behind. The road to Auxerre drove straight up and over four steep wooded hills. It was busy but it had a wide hard shoulder so I slogged slowly up the first climb before launching down the other side – all that effort and not even a gain in altitude before it started again. The big trucks were struggling to find a gear low enough, and I tucked into the right-hand side of the crawler lane, changing into my own granny gear. I concentrated on keeping the pedals turning, and at the top of the climb there was a quick glimpse of hills stretching away north and south before I was sent down into the next town. That was why Columbanus had followed rivers even when he wasn't in a boat.

After two hours of rollercoaster riding I reached Auxerre. Columbanus was here at least once, but long before that the city had played a part in the first solid date in Irish history – in 431 Bishop Palladius was sent from here to minister 'to the Christians in Ireland'. An important town, it had survived the end of Roman control reasonably well, and when Columbanus was here around the turn of the seventh century, its bishop had assumed much of the authority for local government. These 'hunting prelates' had presided over a church that was largely urban, and while there had been a flourishing of monasticism, this, too, was centred in towns (like St Martin's abbey of Marmoutiers in Tours).

I liked the feel of the place so I prescribed myself an afternoon off, and found somewhere to stay. In front of the reception desk in the small hotel I met the largest dog I've ever seen. It resembled a shaggy black pony, but it lumbered around in a gentle fashion and it was a nice change after all the tiny dogs I'd seen elsewhere in France. Otherwise sane men in suits would brazenly walk around town with a dog under one arm, or a petite canine head would stick out of a bag belonging to a woman of a certain age outside a café. In Cancale, I'd seen skate-rat teens out for a night of fun accompanied by their loyal lap-dog. I wasn't sure what to make of all this, but one conclusion was clear – you should never trust a man carrying a dog.

Back out into the steep and winding streets to the abbey of St Germain, and its large collection of Roman artefacts. Statues and funeral steles – built to last – are interesting, but what really took my imagination was the stuff of daily use: spatulas for putting in eye ointment, combs, clasps and tongs, glassware and metal pots. Columbanus had been a lot closer to the Roman period than to the Viking landings in Ireland. He had travelled along Roman roads – the museum had amazing road signs carved in stone – through towns that had been Roman foundations, so this stuff was familiar to him. But the Empire was in tatters and pagan achievements meant little to the Christians of the period. From his writings it's clear that, to Columbanus, Rome meant the Pope and the centre of the Catholic world, not the faded glories of the Empire. But it's easier for modern minds to understand the practical Romans with their engineering projects and ambition for civilisation than to identify with Columbanus and his monastic contemporaries, enduring severe hardship and denial in conditions that seem more primitive than those of Roman times.

In the abbey church our guide led us downstairs into the crypt through layers of history. There were Gallo-Roman columns, sarcophagi from the sixth-century Merovingian church (the time when Columbanus would have been passing through Auxerre), and later Carolingian painted columns and frescoes. Next came the Romanesque and Gothic rebuilding and enlargements. The crypt's columns and arches showed its development through eight centuries. And that still brought me only to the twelfth century. Somewhere in the middle of all that, Columbanus had lived for less than seventy years well over a millennium ago. No wonder it was hard to get a real sense of him even as I passed through places he had been – he was buried in centuries.

Rocky crags were the story of the next day, an overcast Saturday, the first day of September. When he had made the trip in the opposite direction under armed guard, Columbanus arrived in Auxerre from Avallon by sticking to the river valleys of the Cure and the Yonne, but I thought it was worth making a detour to Vézelay – the site of a famous monastery. This was the first day since my arrival in Nantes when I'd been heading south rather than east, and I was in a good mood as I headed up the hill out of Auxerre on the Roman road that Columbanus would have used.

Just as I turned off the road to head towards Vézelay, my mobile phone rang. I'd been carrying it around in the back pocket of my cycling jersey for the whole trip, charging it overnight in my hotel room, and calling friends and family to let them know I was OK. I pulled to the side and answered it: it was my mum, my sister and my two-year-old nephew, just calling to say hello. Young baby Columbanus was fine back in London, and I was in the middle of France on a bike. When I ended the call and looked around me, the landscape suddenly felt more strange, after my temporary transportation to my sister's house and those familiar voices.

I arrived beneath the crag of Vézelay. The road circled round the side of the hill, leading gradually upwards until it reached the village, where it straightened and climbed sharply to the monastery at the summit. It was a painful grind to the top, but there were a few tourists around and I didn't want to get off and push in front of them.

I stopped for a picnic lunch in front of the basilica and, leaving the bike outside the main door, went in when it started to rain. The striped Romanesque columns, the carvings above the doors and the massive scale of the place were all striking, but I was cold and wet and had already ridden fifty hilly kilometres that day so I wasn't in the mood to appreciate it.

I reached the tourist office in busy Avallon tired and concerned. I'd passed a large number of smartly dressed people heading down the pedestrianised main street and disappearing into the church opposite the tourist office. A big wedding in a smallish town on a Saturday night – the hotels might be booked out, and me knackered after all these hills. And so it proved. After three head-shaking rejections at hotels and bars, I ended up at a campsite far below the centre of town. Praise the Lord for enthusiastic Dutch and German campers who keep these sites open in September when the French have all gone back to work.

After a snooze, I found a quick way back up the hill for dinner, served at a cracking pace by a clueless but friendly Victoria Wood lookalike and her accomplice, a sallow youth whose shirt collar was several sizes too big for him.

Back in the tent I settled down to a quick spot of

nocturnal radio listening, to be met with the astonishing news that England had beaten Germany 5–1. With the radio struggling to catch the faintest signals from across the Channel, I listened to English football fans calling in to scream their delight at the result. There was no one to witness my joy and confusion. Ireland had beaten Holland earlier in the day, news I'd met with unalloyed delight. I was at least as Irish as many in the team, and how could you not like the plucky boys in green?

But the Irish part of me could take no satisfaction from an England win. I remember sitting in a Dublin pub watching England playing San Marino in the mid-nineties. The crowd was gathering to watch Ireland's later match, but the loudest cheer of the night came when San Marino scored. I was hugely conflicted. Fortunately, Ireland and England don't play each other very often, so I can normally get by with supporting both teams. And it was the English part of me that was happiest now. I'd been eating mediocre duck when Michael Owen and the others were making history.

11

Dinner from Heaven, Lunch from Hell

A succession of hills was wearing me down. The long drags on the way out of Avallon were just steep enough to have me struggling for the right gear, but when I got to the top, the descents were so mild that I didn't get a smooth coast downhill. The straight line on the map was an example of Roman bloody-mindedness: they'd driven the road across ridge after ridge. I struggled up the climbs, not paying attention to the scenery as the road skirted the national parkland of the Morvan. I got my reward after lunch, with a joyful descent for twenty-five kilometres, and a smart hotel room in Autun as a base for my rest day – 470 kilometres since my last break in Tours.

That evening, at Le Petit Banc, in the rue des Banes, I had a moment. It was a small pizzeria-crêperie in a sloping, cobbled street just down from the cathedral beside an ancient chunk of a museum. The sun was setting as I'd walked up from the hotel, and the surrounding hills were visible from the centre of town. I sat down at one of the tables outside the restaurant. There was an understated style to the menus and the warm, modern room I could see inside. A family who knew the owners were sitting at another table, joking and playing with a smiling toddler. I ordered a salad and some pasta from the funkily clothed waitress. The food and wine were good, but even better was just sitting there after the grind of the day, and after everything that had got me there, with the sun warming the top of the building opposite the restaurant, and the red glow reflecting in the windows. The view down the street was of a succession of old buildings with high windows, and two people walked by carrying violin cases, like they were extras in the movie of my trip. And I was there, a part of it, enveloped in rightness just for a moment.

There's a lot to be said for the elegant formality of French greetings. The next morning I was sitting in a bar on the main square enjoying a creamy *café au lait*. A party of friends was seated at a table opposite me, and as each new person arrived, there was an elaborate round of handshakes and kisses. When the ferry had docked in Roscoff and I'd been in the fume-filled depths waiting for the sign to ride my bike down the ramp, I'd watched the sailors take time to greet their portside colleagues with a handshake. At home you're lucky if you get a nod from your best friend.

I was enjoying my leisurely start to the morning – no tent to pack up, no hours of riding before lunch, and the chance to get a feel for the place. With Dublin losing its charm, I'd been letting my eye wander as I rode through some fetching French towns. Autun was clean, quiet and handsome (a claim not often made for my Dublin neighbourhood), and I imagined what it would be like to live there. This would be where I'd come for coffee, I'd buy bread in that bakery over there, and I'd have one of those chic apartments down that side-street. I knew I'd be on the road to the next town in the morning, but right now Autun looked appealing, and I let myself dream.

The Roman gateway of the Port d'Arroux is on the edge of town near the river. In classical times it marked the north entrance to the town, and it is still in use today. The two larger arches span the modern road, and smaller ones stretch across the pavements on either side. Cars and vans drive through a gate that has stood there for 1800 years. Heading out of town, the road is signed to Saulieu, and it's more than likely that Columbanus walked out of this gate with his armed guard on his way to Avallon. I walked up to the archway and ran my hand over the stone – at last, something that hadn't been covered over by the layers of history, something that the saint and I were seeing in exactly the same way.

Fancying something cheap and cheerful for lunch, I ordered *andouillette* and chips in a bar in town. I thought *andouillette* was a local sausage, but when the meal arrived, I realised I'd made a terrible mistake. The thing that sat there was a loose agglomeration of pork fat, gristle and who knew what else, held together with chopped onions and the will of the devil. It was the same pinkish grey colour that it would be on the way back up, which was appropriate as it already had the consistency of something partly digested. It oozed a watery fat-dappled effluent that soaked into the bottom layer of the chips, and gave off a faintly toxic odour. I scooped up part of it, smothered it with mustard and tried bravely to eat it, but it was no good. My gorge rose in my throat, and I was reduced to picking at the chips that hadn't been contaminated by contact with it. Yesterday's perfect restaurant moment seemed a long time ago.

Up at the cathedral I spent some time examining the carvings above the central door. During the French Revolution, the cathedral canons had plastered over the whole lot, finding them grotesque, and removed the head of Christ because it stuck out too much. The carvings were rediscovered in 1837, but Jesus's head (which spent the nineteenth century in a museum) was not reunited with His body until 1948.

You can see why the canons might have objected to the carvings. All of human life is depicted there, from rich men to thieves, kings to monks, and among the cheeky figures is the image of a pilgrim, identified by his satchel and his conch-shell, showing that he'd been to Santiago de Compostela. My cover as a keen cyclist with an interest in history was wearing thin. I was beginning to realise that I was on a pilgrimage myself. Since Dublin, the book I'd been reading was called *The Art of Pilgrimage*, a selection of quotations and reflections on pilgrims through the ages, from Japan to Peru. It seemed I fitted the profile – I had prepared for my journey by doing lots of studying, it had occurred at a transitional stage in my life, I was following a route laid down for me, it was a challenging and rewarding undertaking, and the journey was as important as the destination. The situation was confused by my suspicion of the Christian faith and my fear of Columbanus, but the book told me that all sorts of people from every faith and none had embarked on pilgrimages, so even though this wasn't what I'd planned, it seemed I might be an accidental pilgrim.

The important thing, apparently, was that the journey revealed things about the pilgrim that had previously been hidden. Under Columbanus's tutelage, I wanted to discover that I was more decisive and strong-willed than I'd thought. I wanted to be a hard-ass like him. But I sensed I was a disappointment as a pupil. A pilgrimage was supposed to be difficult, but I was doing it in a relaxed, easy-going fashion that would cut no ice with the saint. Where was the un-compromising approach he had shown in his journeys? How you travel shows how you live.

Columbanus knew all about an outward journey mirror-ing an inner one, and his surviving sermons are full of refer-ences to the road as a metaphor for life. For him, no one was truly at home on this earth, so whether we walked across a continent or stayed in the village of our birth, we were all fellow pilgrims on the road of life (a phrase that sounds particularly good in Latin: *via vitae*). In one of his sermons he says, 'Then let us who are on the way, hasten home; for our whole life is like the journey of a single day ... and above all let us seek our home [*patriam*]; for the fatherland is where our father is. Thus we have no home on earth, since our father is in heaven.' It's as if all those miles were a physical representation of his journey to God – whatever we thought about our lives, we were all just passing through, so we might as well do that literally.

But Columbanus's relationship with 'home' is problem-atic. From a Christian standpoint, he's arguing that his home is with God, but on a more personal level, he uses the same word, *patriam*, to mean Ireland. As someone who chose exile, perhaps he felt as if he really did have no home on earth, but as one historian has pointed out, 'There is ultim-ately something paradoxical in his personality that remained obstinately Irish in a foreign environment.'

I could identify with him on this point. As an Englishman

just returned from the US to live in Ireland and travel in France, I often felt as if I didn't have a home on earth. Too Irish in England, too English in Ireland, too Euro in the US, too Yankophile in Europe, I was tying myself in knots trying to work out where I should be. No wonder I was falling for every town I came to. The travel writer Bruce Chatwin once described himself as one of those Englishmen who found he could only be English when he wasn't living there. But, then, where's home really?

Maybe Columbanus had realised something I hadn't: that looking for a home anywhere is a mistake. He says, 'Therefore let this principle abide with us, that on the road we so live as travellers, as pilgrims, as guests of the world.' Maybe you should just enjoy the journey on the road of life wherever it takes you. It's a powerful way to live, as a guest of the world. At my best on the trip, when I was only looking at two folds of map a day, I'd stopped worrying and things had become simple again. I hadn't discovered my inner Christian action hero, but perhaps I was learning something.

I'd been on detours before – none of those châteaux along the Loire had had much to tell me about Columbanus – but I'd always been heading in the right direction. Now, the next obvious stop with saintly connections was Chalon-sur-Saône, seat of the Burgundian kings, around eighty kilometres south-east of Autun, but I was taking myself a day out of my way to the south-west to visit that most unlikely thing in the middle of the French countryside: a Buddhist monastery.

Few Christian monasteries in France survived the Revolution and the Napoleonic era, so visiting a Buddhist monastery seemed like the best I could do. Under grey skies I rode out of Autun towards the Temple of a Thousand Buddhas.

After about an hour I followed the signs up a narrow lane, and was deposited in an empty car park. The temple was closed for lunch. I had two hours to wait, and I could see the day drifting away from me. I cracked open my picnic supplies. A British-registered car pulled up, and a family of four got out, the parents trying to tell their young boys that this was a peaceful place so they should probably not run around playing war. I was sitting down near the information sign, so when the father came over I said hello. He looked surprised to be greeted in English.

'I think the temple's closed until two,' I said.

'Oh, right. Where have you come from? Apart from England, I mean.'

'Today, just from Autun, but I've ridden from Dublin in Ireland.'

'Right, right. OK, then. 'Bye.'

I wasn't looking for much reaction to the news that I'd ridden across France, but I'd expected more than 'OK, then'. In true English fashion, it was as if he thought that expressing any interest in my trip would intrude on my privacy. An Irishman would be more likely to congratulate you on the effort, then tell a great yarn about a one-legged friend of his who rode across the Serengeti. It would turn out that his sister had been in your cousin's junior infants class, and half an hour later he'd leave you feeling like he was your new best friend even though he'd told you almost nothing about himself. An American would have shared his uplifting life story with you, in complete medical detail, and told you how neat it was that you had come all this way, even if he couldn't grasp the notion that you didn't have a car. Either approach would have been preferable to the English reluctance to connect on any level.

The family decided it was too long to wait and got back into their car. I finished my lunch and went for a wander round the grounds. Tibetan prayer flags were flying along the paths, and the temple looked like a piece of Asia that had been teleported on to the hillside. A small white *stupa* stood in front of the main building, which reached into the sky with four intricately carved levels coming to a golden point. A little further off stood a compact château. Without the temple, it would have looked perfectly normal in its surroundings but, so close to this amazing structure, it seemed bizarre.

I kicked around some more, and by the time the temple opened, in my head I was already on the road making up for lost time. I was led into an upstairs gallery. From there I could see, in the large hall below, three huge and wonderfully decorated statues. They stretched from floor to ceiling, the central Buddha looking serene and loving. At the side of the gallery there was a large mandala, a circle full of intricately swirling patterns in a delicate range of oranges, reds, yellows and blues. The whole picture, over a metre in diameter, was made from individual grains of sand. It was a beautiful thing. Perhaps even Columbanus would have approved. He expresses a Zen-like awareness of the unreality of the world in which we live, asking, 'What is the difference between what I saw yesterday and what I dreamt this night? Do they not seem to you today to be equally unreal?' Buddhist discipline and commitment to practice would certainly have struck a chord with the saint, who argued, 'Is it not impossible for any polished accomplishment or exercise to be attained without training?'

For Columbanus, this meant self-mortification, and it's easy to think of him only as a drill sergeant, driving his monks to breaking point. But he acknowledges that the physical element is not enough. 'A fruitful moderation of the mind' is also required. The sergeant was also a scholar. This combination of patient practice, physical endeavour and intellectual effort is not too far from Buddhist monastic life, and to me it has an appealing combination of breadth and rigour.

My sixth-form Latin teacher was, to borrow Wolfe Tone's comment about Whitley Stokes, perhaps the best man I have ever met. Mr Cooper used the classics to educate us much more broadly. On my first day in the sixth form, he explained that his aim was to make us see the value of both breadth and rigour in studying Latin. The detail of translation, where every word had to be dissected with rigorous precision, was only as important as the broader understanding of life and literature that reading *The Aeneid* or Horace's poems would give us. In his warm, elegant way he showed us that information was useless without context and that ability was useless without morality. 'Breadth and rigour, gentlemen,' he would say, 'breadth and rigour.'

Columbanus became most attractive to me when I saw him in this light. A scholar who clambered over mountains, a loner who led hundreds of monks, a humble man who corrected popes and kings, and a stern disciplinarian who showed tender compassion to his charges. In a small way, my journey was itself an example of breadth and rigour. Columbanus might not have approved of me, but maybe Mr Cooper would.

★

As I rode away from the monastery, it started to rain. Since I'd left the Loire it had been cloudy almost all the time. I'd worn my leg-warmers every day – in case you think I was riding the roads looking like Leroy from *Fame*, let me explain: cyclists' leg-warmers are tubes of super-technical fleece-lined Lycra, zipped at the bottom, that you slip on to make your shorts into longs. They're the perfect companion to the arm-warmers that beef up your short-sleeved jerseys and have the added benefit of making you look like a professional cyclist. They're modelled by everyone in the pro peloton during the early-season races, and in mountain stages on the big tours. You roll them down to your wrists when you get hot on the climbs, then pull them up for the chilly descent, and suddenly you're Lance Armstrong. Kind of.

The leg-warmers aren't so hip, but they do a great job of keeping your knees and ankles toasty when there's a nip in the air or some light drizzle. But now the rain was so hard that it clattered off the road like marbles. I took shelter under a tree as the shower turned into a full-blown storm and fished in my bag for my clip-on red light – it had got dark and I didn't fancy being flattened by a big truck in the gloom. The rain showed no sign of stopping, and I was already soaked, so I resolved to get moving again. I was a good thirty kilometres from the nearest town, and further from the campsite I'd earmarked for the night. A two-hour soaking and a wet night in a tent didn't sound good, so I went with plan B: any port in a storm. The nearest place was Montceau-aux-Mines, which had been built from scratch in the 1840s when the nearby coalmines had opened. It didn't sound swish, but I was cold and wet and in the middle of nowhere.

I rode out into the teeming rain with my chin pulled down into the collar of my jacket, and a stream of swearing to power me along. The roads weren't steep, but they were naggingly not flat. My expensive 'waterproof' jacket was now shipping water like a rowing-boat rounding Cape Horn, and there was a squelch in each shoe as I turned the pedals. By the time I arrived in Montceau the rain was easing, but I was a sorry sight.

The Grilhotel was a low, roadside block with an East German feel. It was a business hotel, designed for people who had no choice but to be there and weren't paying the bills so didn't care what they got. I checked in, leaving a small puddle beside the front desk. My ground-floor room was institutional, with a view on to the road. But there was plenty of hot water and my *über*-panniers had again survived a serious soaking so I had dry clothes to change into.

That evening I went into the dining room to discover that every one of my fellow diners was male, and more than half were eating alone. This was a sad sight. From my work travel in the US, I knew what it felt like to be one of these sales reps, middle managers or repair-crew members. And, after a flat day, *I* was in a place *I* didn't really want to be, because I, too, was doing a job.

12

Burgundian Reminders

Until now I'd caught up with Columbanus only in places that he'd passed through, but today my lunchtime stop was in Chalon-sur-Saône, seat of the Burgundian royal family who had been Columbanus's mentors and eventual enemies.

It was cold when I left the hotel, but it wasn't raining, and I rode alongside a canal for the first half-hour of the day. Mist hung over the water and fishermen hunched over their rods. The road turned away from the canal towards some rolling hills, and I was convinced I could hear creaking from somewhere on the bike. Apart from cleaning and oiling the chain, and pumping up the tyres, I'd not done any maintenance or repairs, and probably wouldn't be able to if the problem was serious. I promised myself I'd check it at the next stop, and tried not to worry about it. At major points in the day – reaching twenty-five or fifty kilometres, for example – I patted the handlebars and said well done to it (and to myself), but that wouldn't fix a worn-out bottom bracket.

That I was talking to the bike shouldn't come as a surprise. Lasting relationships are forged while you're cycling. You and your bike remain static while the landscape slides by, so the bicycle is the only thing you can have a discussion with. I hadn't named my steed, but felt guilty that it was still just a Dawes Horizon. It's like calling your dog Black Labrador. But if it was going to have a name, it had to be something traditionally English, like Albert or George. In contrast, my American-made mountain bike would have had a radical name like Rip or Clint, and it would be too cool to talk to me.

As I came down the hill into the town of Buxy, the broad Saône river valley opened up and vineyards appeared for the first time since Orléans. There is little left in Chalon to show its former royal status, but it's likely that Columbanus first came here to petition King Sigebert for some land on which to found a monastery. Jonas, perhaps deliberately, gives us the wrong king's name but describes the meeting in detail: 'When the holy man with his companions appeared before the king, the greatness of his learning caused him to stand high in the favour of the king and court.'

This is probably close to the truth, as Columbanus's command of Latin, the scriptures and exegesis was excellent, and it would have been considered a great benefit to have such a devout and learned man on your payroll. Sigebert offered Columbanus money to stay at court, and when the monk demurred, offered him a hermitage instead. He proposed a spot 'in the great wilderness called Vosagus [the Vosges] in which there was a fortress which had long been in ruins'. For the Irish monks, consorting with royalty was not as unusual as it sounds. Christianity was a high-class calling at home, and Columbanus would have been familiar with royal patronage of monasteries. As one historian has pointed out, monks at the time were 'men of power … not the misfits, the naturally humble and retiring, they were the social élite'.

While he was considering this offer, Columbanus didn't contact the religious authorities in Burgundy. Although the collapse of Roman control and the invasion of the Franks had undoubtedly done a great deal of damage in Gaul, there was still a Catholic infrastructure throughout the country, with priests, metropolitan bishops and a thriving monastic culture. However, it was largely centred on the former Roman towns, and its make-up and attitudes would have seemed strange to Columbanus, coming from a country that didn't even have any towns. In his later letters, it is clear that he felt the bishops were at best less rigorously devout than he would have liked, and at worst heretical simoniacs who had turned away from the true teachings of Rome. We'll see what the bishops thought of him soon enough, but Columbanus seems simply to have wanted a place in the country to found a monastery like the ones he had known at home.

I'd been in Burgundy before, under different circumstances. One day, as an impoverished master's student during my first year in Dublin, I'd been munching a bar of Aero chocolate to fuel my essay on obscure Irish modernist poets. There was a competition on the wrapper: you had to answer three simple questions about French food and drink, and write a tie-breaker. The prize was a gourmet week in Paris and Dijon. I wasn't getting far with the essay so I started pondering the tie-breaker (to be completed in less than ten words): 'Aero is a part of a gourmet life because…' There was only one way to go with this: punning, rhyming French. My killer entry went: '*C'est magnifique, c'est fantastique, c'est AERO-dynamique!*'

I'm ashamed to say that I won. Or, rather, I would be ashamed, but the prize was so fantastic that I didn't care what I'd had to do to get it. With perhaps nine other winners (and their guests), I and a gastronaut fellow student from Portadown were flown from Dublin to Paris. There, we were wined and dined for a couple of days before we caught the TGV to Dijon for trips to vineyards and lavish restaurants, and ended up at a château for a seven-course feast. The other winners were all serious competition entrants, and when I told them this was the first (and last) competition I'd ever entered, they treated me like an *idiot savant* with an amazing gift for cheesy tie-breakers. Some of the compers wouldn't even tell me what their winning entry had been but they all had a few examples of classic slogans. In the pantheon of tie-breakers, one in particular stood out, a winning entry for a car in a competition organised by a chicken company: 'I'd look good in a new Fiesta from Moy Valley Chickens because it's poultry in motion!'

The competition entrants came from all over Ireland and from all walks of life, and they all denied being serious about their hobby. But then they'd tell you how their children didn't go to the cinema with them any more because they made them root through the bins to pick out discarded chocolate wrappers. One man let slip that he'd go down to Lansdowne Road after a rugby or football international so he could pick up the crisp packets dropped by the departing fans. When I told my friends I'd won, they all said, 'Wow, I've never won anything in my life,' and now you know why – the same group of committed competition freaks hoovers up every prize because they want it so much more than you do.

The Burgundy trip was a delight, although I was uneasy that Nestlé were paying for everything, given their tarnished reputation from their baby-milk operations in Third-World countries. I benefited from their largesse while vowing never to eat another Aero. Exactly where we went in the Burgundy area is something of a blur, as I was pickled with Meursault, Nuits St George and kir royale the whole time, but when I looked at the maps now, some names seemed familiar so I skirted the most popular destinations on my way eastwards.

In the afternoon I arrived in the small village of Seurre, on the Saône river east of Beaune. Even though it was still only early September, the campsite shop and swimming-pool had been closed, and it was winding down for the season. I chose a spot beside the river, near an elderly Swiss couple with a meticulous caravan. In the only restaurant in the village, a young couple ate their way through a three-course dinner in complete silence. I spoke more than they did, and I was on my own. An older German couple got up to leave, and a golden retriever uncurled himself from under the table and padded out quietly with them. I hadn't even known he was there.

You wouldn't get that sort of obedience from a French dog. As well as the continuing ridiculousness of the lapdogs, I'd been barked at by yappy terriers and maladjusted poodles every day since Roscoff. Most of the time they saw me coming and dashed over to the fence that separated their garden from the road. I just prayed that there was never a hole for them to escape through, and I'd only been chased once. It didn't seem to matter if you were riding the bike or not, just being a cyclist was enough: in rainy Montceau, a dog had gone mad at me just for wheeling the bike down the street.

★

Buddhists do walking meditations. I do cycling meditations. Before I left home I was worried that spending all this time on my own would threaten my sanity, and since I've returned people have asked me what I was thinking about while I was on the bike. The answer is that I can't really say, and that's what kept me sane. I wasn't thinking about riding in a straight line, or changing gear or drinking from my water-bottles, because I did all that automatically. When there were cars around, or difficult junctions to negotiate, I was certainly concentrating, but not with the kind of rational concentration that comes out as sentences in your head. Judging how fast a car is approaching, or tucking in when a lorry goes past requires a different sort of awareness – you're paying attention, but if you're asking yourself, 'Is it OK for me to go now, do you think?' you're acting too slowly.

But every pedal-turn showed me something new, and as I went by I was looking at the scenery, the dead bird on the road, the road signs, the houses, the windows of the houses, the paint peeling on the frame of the upstairs window above the door… These snapshots filled my head and combined with the feel of the air, the wind, the road surface, the colour of the light. I was processing a lot of data.

I was also singing. A playlist of appropriate songs developed first in my head, and then at the back of a notebook. I sang aloud, or just played a song to myself internally. When I hear them now the dozen or so tracks that were on heavy rotation during the trip still make me smile and think of France.

Sometimes on quiet roads, I'd drift off through corridors of my brain that I'd not been down in years. Odd details from events I'd all but forgotten would appear on the surface, sharp as a bright winter's day. Or solutions to problems would arrive unbidden. The constant chattering in my head was stilled by the cycling, and I was left much more open – aware of things without concentrating on them, reminded of things without thinking about them, and singing like a loon.

The following morning there were some lovely kilometres, with the sun shining on smooth and quiet roads through rich farmland. I stopped at one point to photograph a tree-lined stretch that looked just too perfect. The market was packing up in front of the cathedral as I rode into Dole, the home of Louis Pasteur. I wolfed down a sandwich sitting on a wall beside the front of a college. Coolly dressed teenagers were being dropped off by their parents for afternoon classes, and the kids couldn't get out of the cars fast enough, trying to avoid an embarrassing embrace. When you're seventeen, parents are like spots – everyone's got them, but you try to pretend they don't exist.

The terrain was getting more hilly again, which limited the number of alternative routes I could take. On flat plains, countless smaller roads meandered through the countryside, making it possible to get to even the larger towns without having to take the main road. But for most of that afternoon I was jostled by cars and sucked at by the backdraught of trucks. The first chance I got, I pulled off the main road, and tried to find the back door into Besançon. I was in a very small village named St Vit, and there was only one way out of it that wasn't the main road, but I still had to ride round the place three times before I found it.

With the skies darkening again, I approached Besançon. The centre of the city sits with a rocky crag behind it, and a wide loop of the Doubs river in front. I reached the river, looked across at the old town, with its fortifications on top of the hill, and knew that I was close to the tourist office. I had a map showing its location, just a couple of bridges down the river. But then I saw a sign pointing to it in the opposite direction. I trusted the road signs, not the map, and was led away from the centre of town on to dual carriageways, back towards the centre, over at least one bridge, into the citadel, back out again, and beyond where I'd originally stopped. Tired and annoyed, it dawned on me that I was following instructions meant for cars in the complex one-way system. It would have been quicker to walk from where I had started. I finally arrived at the tourist office, which was about 150 yards away from where I'd first come in.

13

The Prison-Break Saint

Miracles were the stock in trade of medieval saints. It was how they got the job in the first place, and Columbanus was no exception to the rule. He healed people, made food appear, had a way with wild animals and the gift of prophecy. But to ensure his tough-guy image, he also performed a prison-break miracle. Right here in Besançon.

I was tired after my slogging day, but I had to explore the scene of this excitement, so I dumped my things at a hotel off the Grande Rue and headed out. The town is still much the same as Jonas described it: 'so situated that the houses are clustered together on the sides of a steep mountain. Above, the lofty cliffs rise perpendicularly into the heavens. The mountain is cut off on all sides by the river.'

After a particularly angry dispute with King Theuderic, soldiers arrested Columbanus and brought him to the city. It's not clear if he was imprisoned, but he visited the prison and preached to the condemned men. They promised to mend their ways, and when Columbanus's attendant picked up their iron shackles they 'broke into bits like the rotten trunk of a tree'. The saint told them to rush to the church to do penance.

We don't know where the prison was, but there are two

main candidates for the church, both of which are still used as places of worship. The church of St Pierre is about halfway along the Grande Rue, the Roman main street of the city, while the cathedral is to the south, closer to the crag. When the released prisoners reached the church they found the doors locked, but with soldiers approaching them, it was time for another miracle. Columbanus opened the doors, then closed them behind the prisoners to give them time to escape through the back. The soldiers found the doorkeeper, whom Jonas names as Aspasius, but even with the key 'he said he had never found them more tightly closed'. The redeemed prisoners made good their escape.

Columbanus remained in Besançon for a time, but after the miracles, no one was going to give him a hard time. One Sunday he clambered up to the top of the crag for a look round. On his way up, he passed a Roman triumphal arch that still stands near the cathedral. As I'd done in Autun, I put my hand to the stone that Columbanus would have seen, then set off after him up the steep slope. From the top, the city stretched out below me, and the Grande Rue ran straight towards the bridge and out of the citadel. Columbanus waited until noon to see if anyone would stop him returning to his monastery, then 'took the road leading directly through the city' and headed home.

I was tired and hungry, but couldn't find a restaurant. Eventually I stumbled into a square full of wooden stalls offering local delicacies, from wine and cheese to cakes and pastries. I passed a baker's stall, and was struck by the small dark-haired woman behind the counter. She was chatting to a customer, and her lustrous eyes and cheeky smile were matched only by the quality of her baked goods. I walked up to the counter, and before I could think of anything smart to say to her, it was my turn. I reddened and pointed towards the *pains aux pommes*.

'*Ah, ils sont très bons. Vous voulez combien?*' A smile played around her lips, and she might as well have been asking me to marry her. Suddenly I imagined living in an apartment above the bakery, waking to the smell of fresh baguettes and the noise of *ma femme la boulangère* working below me. We would be conjoined in breaded bliss.

It was a symptom of the conditional nature of my life that I was so susceptible to the innocent charms of the women I met. I didn't know where I wanted to live, what I wanted to do, or with whom I wanted to do it. I was drowning in uncertainty and was looking to anyone I thought might throw me a line. A more confident man might have left a trail of conquests across France. But all I could do was meekly ask for a loaf of apple bread and slide off thinking of what might have been. I drowned my sorrows with a half-bottle of buttery chardonnay in a restaurant beside the square, then retired to my room well-fed but alone.

Besançon proved no easier to leave than it had been to enter, and I narrowly avoided joining the A36 motorway to Paris. There were roadworks on the N road north to Vesoul, and I got to see them laying the black, fine-grained Euromacadam close up. Irish road surfaces are improving, but they're still a long way from this lovely stuff. Car drivers experience different amounts of road noise depending on the quality of the road they're on, and the odd pothole might make their suspension work a little, but for a cyclist, a choppy surface means harder work and a more painful ride, while potholes can puncture tyres and bend wheels. Bad surfaces are also unsafe, especially when you're coming down steep hills at speed on skinny wheels. Our only suspension is a little give in the wheels, maybe some flex in the frame and the padding in our gloves. Elbows work like shock absorbers, and for really rough stuff we'll be out of the saddle so the bike can bounce around without beating us up too much. The smooth Euromacadam made it possible to ride more quickly, comfortably and safely.

As soon as I could, I veered off on to quieter roads and saw my first cows with bells round their necks. Timber-framed houses were appearing, and there was a growing Alpine tinge to the landscape. The hills weren't mountains yet, but I sped down a long descent into busy Vesoul, situated next to a lake. I set up the tent at the modern and largely empty campsite. There had been no repeat of the creaking I thought I'd heard from the bike, but I'd noticed that the steering was a little graunchy. Now I checked it: there was clearly something wrong with the headset – where the front fork and handlebar stem meet the frame. The poor bike needed professional care. If it got me to Luxeuil, I'd book it in for treatment.

As a hungry cyclist in a land of late diners, I'd got used to eating in quiet restaurants, but the lakeside place I chose tested to the full my immunity to embarrassment. I took my place in the deserted room, close to the window so I wouldn't have to look at all the empty tables. It was still early, and I was sure the place would fill up – it was Friday, after all.

As a solo diner, the major hurdle to overcome is the staff's view of you as a pathetic Johnny-no-mates. They'll put you at the most out-of-the-way table because they don't want to be known as the establishment where sad people eat. Then they'll get you out as quickly as possible – they only get half the tip for the same number of visits to the table so you're not worth the effort.

During my first two courses the waitress tactfully withdrew to the kitchen. I could hear the cooks singing along to U2. When it became clear that I was going to be the only customer all night, I didn't have the heart to order dessert and made it back to the tent early to prepare for the excitement of tomorrow.

14

In Columbanus's Town

It had just started raining on the Saturday lunchtime shoppers outside the restaurant, but I didn't care. I was almost in tears as I scribbled in my notebook:

> *Very worried something bad would happen at the last. The skies were so heavy you could cut the clouds with a knife and fork. But it had been a windy and warm night and the tent was dry as I packed up. Out through the hills on edge of Vesoul, then more up and down, with wooded tops to the hills. As I came down the hill just after Nourey-en-Vaux I saw the wooded folds of the landscape stretch on and on. Soon after I saw my first sign for Luxeuil and let out a whooping holler.*

I took a photograph of myself in front of the Luxeuil sign on the edge of town – another classic cyclist-with-sign pose. As I turned on to the sloping main street, I saw the church of Columbanus's monastery. I'd been riding badly all morning, the bike was aching, and it was raining, but it didn't matter. I'd made it to Luxeuil, 1793 kilometres since leaving my house in Dublin.

After lunch, I checked into my hotel. It was up past the

casino, which sounds more glamorous than it was, a non-descript grey building that doubled as the local cinema. I got directions to the bike shop, where an open-faced mechanic with blue overalls and a messy shock of blond hair examined my sturdy Dawes. The graunchy headset was serious, but he could fix it. Only not until Tuesday lunchtime, as they were closed on Monday, and today he was busy.

I left my bike in the shop, walked back down to the main street and had a coffee across from Columbanus's church. The doctor and his wife were in the corner, their big Saab parked outside, and two farm-hands at the bar were joking with the landlady over an early Kronenbourg. A couple of stray German tourists were sheltering from the rain at a table next to an elderly couple with their shopping, and two miserable-looking teenagers in black Limp Bizkit T-shirts were playing the *Star Wars* pinball machine. You only get this sort of mingling in small towns – in a larger one, everyone would have found their own place to hang out.

Luxeuil is a quiet country town with squat buildings on the narrow main street, which quickly gets clogged with traffic when someone stops outside the post office, or a lorry arrives to restock the fancy opticians that every French town seems to have. But it has some historic sites, and an existence as a spa town that stretches back to Roman times. There are still thermal baths near the casino, and the main street used to be lined with lacemakers, selling their delicate wares to the well-off ladies who arrived by train for a cure. Today its best days might be behind it – several of the formerly grand hotels are boarded up – but I felt comfortable there. After all, Irish people had been arriving since around 590, when Columbanus and his followers fetched up in this wooded country.

Columbanus is everywhere. There are streets named for him, the local dry-cleaner's is 'Pressing S. Colomban' – the saint was famed for the sharp crease in his habit – and even the lingerie shop carries his name (although I'm not sure he'd appreciate that). I crossed the square and walked up to the statue of him outside the church. 'How are you doing?' I said to him. 'I've come a long way to see you.' He didn't say anything, but he looked suitably stern, quite unlike the gentle statue in St Coulomb. He has his right arm raised as if to smite someone, and in the outstretched left he carries a long staff. He's looking down, his face fixed in righteous anger as he towers over you. I felt like some poor monk who'd fallen asleep during mass.

I wasn't the first visitor from Ireland to admire the statue by sculptor Claude Grange. Twenty thousand people attended its unveiling on 23 July 1950, including Éamon de Valera, the then Taoiseach John A. Costelloe, and Seán McBride, minister for external affairs. Also present were the papal nuncio for France, who was to become Pope John XXIII, and Robert Schumann, the French minister for foreign affairs. In his speech on that day Schumann said, 'St Columbanus is the patron saint of those who seek to construct a united Europe,' which sounds like an anachronism of the highest order, but has some truth to it: the saint was a proud member of a powerful pan-European organisation with a centralising attitude and a presence in every corner of the continent – the Catholic Church predates the EU by nearly two millennia, but there are parallels between the two.

Inside the organisation's branch office in Luxeuil – the parish church – there are other more conventional representations of the saint in statue form and stained glass. There's a visitors' book opposite a side chapel dedicated to Columbanus, and I wrote my name and a few lines about how I'd ridden from Bangor following his route. I was walking out again when a young woman stopped me, and asked in halting English if I was the *monsieur* who had written in the book. She was from Luxeuil, but was now living in Strasbourg, and she was just back for the weekend. 'You come from Ireland? It is a good thing you do,' she said.

'Thank you. I'm very pleased to be here.'

'You have seen Sonia in the office of tourism?'

'Not yet.'

'Ah, you should go to see her.'

Sonia looked like a trendy art teacher at a sixth-form college, with a well-tailored black jacket, black bobbed haircut, and a smart blouse-and-scarf ensemble. It was nearly closing time, but when she heard I'd come from Ireland, she found all sorts of documentation for me, and promised to arrange a tour of the abbey, which is now a private Catholic school. If I dropped in on Monday morning, she'd let me know if she'd found a guide. After drifting through town after town leaving no trace, it was great to have an appointment.

That night I ate in a small upmarket restaurant, and was served by a team of staff because it was a quiet night. The proprietor, an upright, serious man in his thirties, had once been on a fishing trip to Belturbet in County Cavan, and he became the next person to hear my story. After not talking to anyone for so long, I'd become positively loquacious since arriving in Luxeuil: the woman in the basilica, the bike mechanic, Sonia and now the restaurateur – I'd told them all about my trip, and it felt great, as if they'd been waiting for me. When I left, we shook hands – the first time I'd taken part in the formal French ritual.

From my hotel-room window I could see the illuminated top of the basilica, on the site of Columbanus's abbey church. I sifted through my papers, and found my material on Margaret Stokes: the Irish artist and antiquarian had visited Luxeuil in April 1893 in search of traces of the saint. She delights a little too much in telling the story of the sack of the Roman town by barbarians in 451:

> *The moat was filled up, the walls scaled, and the Huns, masters of the city, giving the reins to their wild passions, pitilessly massacred the inhabitants, burnt their temples and broke their idols … soon all traces of culture, science, art and even religion disappeared, while the people roamed half naked among the wreck, and still trembled at the name of Attila.*

A hundred and fifty years later, Columbanus founded three monasteries in the area, the first a few miles east in a place called Annegray, the second and largest in Luxeuil, and the third in the village of Fontaines, to the north of the town. There's also a cave in the steep hills near Annegray that is traditionally described as his retreat. I was going to visit all the outlying sites, but would have to wait until Tuesday when my bike was fixed. But I had to be up early in the morning for Sunday mass. I'd been in lots of churches since I arrived in France, but now I felt I should really go to church.

It was a hard life for the monks who lived under Columbanus. In the early years of the monasteries, there seems to have been a constant shortage of food. The monks had to grow or make everything they needed, although Jonas records some examples of generosity from local inhabitants. During the day, most of the brothers would be working in the fields or sent to catch fish from the rivers. The Rule they lived by was very strict, and one historian has described how Jonas 'gives a convincing picture of Columbanus's intense spirituality, based on total subjugation to the will of God ... and of a personal magnetism that inevitably seemed to have a supernatural basis: the moments of percipience and gentleness do much to mitigate the impression of unreasoning and unreasonable harshness given by the disciplinary provisions of rights and penitentials.'

For a young monk, it must have seemed that Columbanus was both good cop and bad cop. Jonas relates how a brother working in the fields cut his finger with a sickle so that it 'hung on by only a small strip of skin'. The saint rushed to him and restored the finger with application of his holy saliva. Other miracles have him providing food and drink for his hungry students, and stopping the rain so they could get the harvest in.

But you had to deserve healing. Once, when he found many brethren ill at Luxeuil, Columbanus commanded them to rise from their beds and thresh the grain. Those who struggled to their feet and made an effort were cured, but those who couldn't get up were cursed to a long continuance of their illness to show them the inadequacy of their faith. Jonas declares this to be 'wonderful revenge. For the disobedient were so ill for an entire year that they barely escaped death.'

Columbanus was stern, but he led by example. Jonas says that often he would retreat to the forest to fast and devote himself to prayer: 'He was so attenuated with fasting that he scarcely seemed alive.' Columbanus himself argued, 'He spurns the world who conquers himself, who dies to his vices before he dies by nature.' This is clearly a kind of sado-monasticism, but his caring side is also shown in his letters and sermons, and one list of wise exhortations shows a more flexible side than we might expect:

Be helpful in humbleness, and most lowly in authority; simple in faith and trained in character; exacting in your own affairs and unconcerned in those of others; hard in times of ease and easy in times of hardness; flexible in even circumstances and even in changeable ones; slow in anger and swift to learn; friendly to the upright, rough to the dishonourable; gentle to the weak and firm to the stubborn.

As the trip went on, I was finding a few chinks in Columbanus's armour. He was still the zealot he'd always been, but it was nice to know he could be human sometimes. His steely determination and drive didn't seem to be rubbing off on me, but maybe my flexibility was rubbing off on him.

Sunday mass, and the congregation in Columbanus's abbey church looked a lot like the one in Dunshaughlin, County Meath. Despite being nominally Anglican, I'd been to many more Catholic services than C of E ones, during holidays with my Irish family. Once, a young cousin had burst into tears at the thought that I was going to go to hell because as a heathen Englishman I didn't take Catholic communion. The congregation here in Luxeuil were either pensioners or young couples with children under twelve. As befitted coun-try folk, the men were wearing patterned jumpers in muted earth tones, and nobody's Sunday best was all that good. The animated choirmaster kept turning round to encourage the congregation in the singing, and I tried to join in.

After the sermon, the choir sang a psalm and the hairs stood up on the back of my neck. In exactly the same place fourteen hundred years ago, Columbanus and his monks had devoted much of their time to the psalms. We can build up a picture of their practices from the Rules he wrote for his French monasteries. There were eight daily offices, and during daylight hours the monks were excused long observances because they were working in the fields. At night, however, the monastery would wake every three hours, and file into the chapel to sing psalms. In the longer nights of the winter there was more singing, and one historian has worked out that on certain holy days the monks sang half of the psalter, or seventy-five psalms. Then they went back to sleep for an hour before getting up and doing it again. There, in the successor to his own church listening to the psalm, I was doing something of which Columbanus might have approved.

After the service I called into the museum, housed in a late medieval fortified tower. The curator was chain-smoking behind a trestle table with a metal cashbox in front of him. He apologised profusely for his bad English, then went on to describe in perfect technical vocabulary the many Roman funeral steles and busts arranged in the room. The museum was a bit ramshackle, but the impressive artefacts had all been found in the area.

Upstairs I found a bust of an imperious-looking young man with curly hair and a handsome gaze. Margaret Stokes had toured the Luxeuil collection of Gallo-Roman remains, and picked out a bust for an extended examination. Perhaps this was the man who had prompted her to write,

There is a story in the face that might appeal to any earnest man, irrespective of his creed. If Columban saw this face, and the thing is not impossible, was his untrained eye wholly incapable of beholding in its expression that which might indeed have awakened his deepest sympathy? The profound sadness born of the failure of all earthly hope, the earnest searching after a higher revelation, seem to have left their mark here. If he saw this laurel-crowned head, half-hidden in the ruins of the gymnasium, did he only rank it with those other statues that he speaks of as 'objects of wretched worship and profane rites'? Or did he behold the struggle in which he was engaged under a new and different light? Here, his was the rude, untutored mind, as compared with that before him. And yet in his heart lay the power that was to satisfy those yearnings, and bring hope where despair had entered in.

Stokes was clearly more artist than historian – 'the profound sadness born of the failure of all earthly hope' is a lot to get from a bust. But you can forgive the sleight-of-hand over whether or not Columbanus would have seen this piece because she's making a fascinating point: she feels she has much more in common with the civilised Romans than with the 'rude, untutored mind' of Columbanus. But, of course, the Romans as she imagines them were inconveniently pagan, while her poor Dark Ages countryman was Christian, if a little unkempt. So she smudges the differences between the two by suggesting that Columbanus would have recognised that this man, though a pagan, was 'searching after a higher revelation' just as he was.

Stokes stresses that the saint's power came from this 'heart'. It was a given of the late-nineteenth-century Celtic Revival movement to which Stokes belonged that these shadowy figures were passionate and primal, in contrast to the desiccated over-rational inhabitants of the modern world. Of course, in reality, Columbanus wrote excellent Latin, and while he wasn't well versed in the classics of Latin literature, he had a profound and scholarly knowledge of things that were important to running a monastery. In Stokes's description of the saint studying the Roman bust she clearly wants the Roman to be a little more Christian, and the Christian to be a little more Roman – or perhaps for them both to be a little more like her, a pious Church of Ireland lady in her sixties who was steeped in Virgil and Horace.

But I can't be too hard on her – she came all this way on her own and found there wasn't much to see when she arrived. In a letter to one of her friends, she says, 'I confess to feeling some disappointment at finding how few and far between are any Christian monuments here that can be said to belong to the period of Columban's sojourn in this country.' Certainly the church now in Luxeuil is of much later construction, and there's no trace of the rest of the abbey, largely due to the success the foundation enjoyed: it was in continuous use for over a thousand years, survived its share of fires and riots, not to mention attacks from the Moors and Normans, and was rebuilt many times.

I adjourned to the hotel, and noticed grey bags under my eyes. Since my digestive adventure along the Loire, I'd had no further health problems, but reaching my first real goal had made me relax, and now I felt very tired. I lay down on the bed and slept deeply for two hours. I woke a little bewildered, and switched on the television to see a perfect American small-town main street – cars were parked at angles outside small Mom-and-Pop stores, the high blue sky seemed to go on for ever, and the confident people glowed with health. My heart ached for the luxury of wholesome consumption and perfect teeth. What was I doing in the middle of nowhere in France? I should never have left the US. I could be there now, driving with the top down to a baseball game in the golden Midwestern sun.

I felt I'd been cursed with all my mind-expanding travel. What was the good of feeling comfortable in northern California, or west Cork, or eastern France when there was nowhere you felt completely at home? I was stranded on the road of life. Having friends all over the place meant that you were always saying goodbye to someone. Surely it shouldn't be so easy to get on my bike and ride across a country? Shouldn't I have more ties and commitments to weigh me down, stop me drifting off? Columbanus had had a weight and purpose that still made him a substantial figure fourteen hundred years after he died. Maybe this long and difficult journey wasn't a pilgrimage but a distraction from the realisation that I still had no idea what I was going to do when I got back.

15

Changed Utterly

You know you're in a small town when you've only been there two days and you keep bumping into people you recognise. The previous night, in the town's only Chinese restaurant, I'd met the proprietor of the restaurant from the night before. Now it was Monday afternoon and I'd arrived at the tourist office for my tour of the abbey to be met by the museum curator, still chain-smoking and wrapped up in a long scarf against the chilly weather.

My guide this morning was the local amateur historian, a bright-eyed elderly man named Monsieur Vidal.

Sonia had taken me under her wing, and she was bustling around, appearing with a poster for me and some cherries in a jar – a local delicacy. I thought we were all set to head over to the abbey, when a photographer arrived. 'It's for the local newspaper,' Sonia explained. 'I have told them of your adventure. Is that good?'

'Fantastic,' I said.

We lined up and the picture was taken. This was fun. A celebrity cyclist-historian – maybe it could work after all. But then I remembered that I should have talked to a few more people on the way, to fill the book with enough material. I'd have to come up with some digressions or something. I had a scholar's disease: I was in my head a lot, and when I realised (in my head) that I was too much in my own head, it just made me worry some more (in my own head). Where was Columbanus when I needed him to bash some sense into me?

The abbey was much more school than religious site, and the smell of overcooked vegetables wafted through the run-down corridors. The polite pupils made way for us as we walked around, but there was little to see. I spent the rest of the afternoon in a café, poring over my guidebooks and maps of Switzerland. When I left Luxeuil I was only going to be two days from the Swiss border and I needed to plan my stops. This practical work made the new country seem more accessible, and I was less troubled by my earlier misgivings about unwelcoming Germanic souls wielding *bratwurst*. Now I was curious to see what it was like.

I adjourned to the hotel, and was scribbling some notes when the phone rang. It was Sonia: would I be free tomorrow for another photograph and press interview, this time with the biggest regional paper, *L'Est Republicain*? Of course.

The next morning I put on my smart green shirt, which I'd brought with me for just such an eventuality, and strolled down to the tourist office. It was quite a party – Fabrice the journalist was a large, shambling, tousle-haired man, who looked like Gerard Depardieu (Gerry Jeopardy, as my Portadown gastronaut friend calls him). Monsieur Vidal, Sonia and her colleague Virginie were all there, and they were joined by their boss Jean-Claude, a small, dapper man and fellow cyclist. First we had a photograph outside the office, with Jean-Claude giving me a Luxeuil T-shirt, then assembled round the large table at the back while Virginie went to make coffee.

My interview was to be a spectator sport, and I wasn't sure my French was up to it. I'd been a journalist in a former life, and it felt peculiar being on the other side of the notebook, especially in the wrong language. We all needed those earpieces they use in the UN, with a bank of interpreters behind us.

First we got the basic facts out of the way, and then we were on to the good stuff.

'Is this a spiritual journey?'

I did my best French shrug, and tried to explain that while I wasn't a practising Christian, I was beginning to feel that there was a spiritual dimension to the trip.

'What was St Columbanus like?'

I'd been waiting for this one, so I had my French all lined up and ready to go: *'Il était un homme très difficile, mais je pense qu'il était un proto-Européen. Il a été en Irlande, en France, en Suisse et en Italie, et pour lui, les similarités sont plus importantes que les différences.'* A proto-European? That wasn't even English, so it was definitely not good French, but I thought the 'similarities more important than the differences' cliché should work OK.

It felt like I was on one of the intellectual discussions I'd seen on French television. The crowd nodded sagely, so I continued to mangle the language trying to explain that I'd just come back from America, where everything was new. *'C'est très intéressant voyager dans l'histoire et aussi dans la France,'* I schmoozed, hoping a good soundbite would overcome bad grammar.

One question Fabrice didn't ask was whether I was mad.

They accepted my journey as an understandable thing for a young man to do, which was refreshing, especially as I couldn't shake my own suspicion that I was a couple of spokes short of a wheel. My internal critic repeated the questions I'd been asked by my Irish and English friends: 'That's all very well, David, but why, exactly?' 'Do you not think it's a bit of an odd idea?' Somewhere in their reaction I liked to see a certain wistfulness, as if they, too, would like to do something like this but wouldn't allow themselves, but it's as likely they just had more sense than me. Either way, my new French friends made me feel like I wasn't mad, which meant a lot.

We finished our short, sharp coffees and I arranged to meet Fabrice at the Columbanus statue with my bike for another photo. I nipped up the road to the bike shop, where my steed had been expertly repaired and tweaked for the equivalent of three pounds. Result.

Back at the hotel, I threw on cycling clothes and stuffed some kit into my panniers to make them look full. Down again to the church for the photograph of me standing behind my bike with Columbanus looming large over my head. This somehow made the trip official.

In the afternoon, the ride to Annegray was pleasant after a few days off the bike. It was a warm afternoon, and the sun was trying to come out – a welcome change after the cold and damp weather of the previous two weeks. The hills on either side of the road got higher and steeper, until they stood up from the flat valley floor like green walls. A few kilometres before Annegray I spotted a sign to Columbanus's retreat. Jonas tells of the abbot regularly taking

himself away from the monasteries for some quiet contem-
plation in a cave, and for centuries the local story has been
that this was where he came.

As the road turned uphill into the woods, it became a
track, then a muddy footpath. I kept on pedalling. Suddenly
I was in a clearing with a small grey stone chapel in front of
a rock outcrop. Beside the chapel there was a fissure in the
rock, where two slabs had pulled away from each other,
creating a narrow cave. I could hear running water, and a
little way down from the cave a small spring emptied into a
rectangular stone trough. Across the clearing a tall Celtic
cross stood looking down to the valley.

It was a peaceful place, with a few birds singing, and a
soft wind nudging the trees. When Columbanus first came
here, he found a bear living in the cave and ordered her to
leave. Jonas's *Life* is full of stories of how well Columbanus
got on with wildlife. Jonas says he was often to be seen
wandering in the woods, 'calling the wild beasts and the
birds. These came immediately at his command and he
stroked them with his hand. The beasts and birds joyfully
played, frisking about with him, just as cats frisk with their
mistresses.'

The gentler side of Columbanus is particularly associated
with his time alone in the wilderness, and reflects a broader
appreciation for nature in the early Irish church. Monks
scribbled short poems in the margins of the manuscripts
they were copying, describing what they saw out of the
scriptorium window, or in one case giving a pen portrait of
an individual monk's cat. One eighth- or ninth-century
epigram records a blackbird's song: 'The little bird has given
a whistle from the tip of its bright yellow beak. The blackbird

from the yellow-tufted bough sends forth its call over Loch Loigh.' (Another piece of marginalia describes a different sort of attractive bird: 'I do not know with whom Edan will sleep, but I do know that fair Edan will not sleep alone.') These flashes of immediacy are some of the first examples of written Irish, and it can be argued that the monks' affinity with the natural world came from the pagan traditions that were still strong in Ireland. It's no accident that Columbanus founded all his monasteries in rural areas, and for him God was in all things. In one of his sermons, he advises, 'Understand the creation if you wish to know the Creator.'

The sun came out as I entered the small chapel – just two rows of benches, and a white marble altar with some fading flowers in a vase. There was a school exercise book for visitors on a side table, and I wrote the date – 11 September 2001 – and my name and address below the others and went to look at the cave. A jam-jar of blue forget-me-nots shone in the dark grey shadows of the narrow opening. I ducked my head, and shuffled inside. There was very little space, just enough room for a man to lie down. Water gurgled some-where below. When Columbanus was first staying in the cave, his serving-boy Domoalis had brought water up to him along the narrow tracks. One day he complained about the effort involved, and Columbanus told him to make a little hole in the back of the cave. The boy obeyed, and a stream of water appeared. As Jonas says, 'The water began to flow regularly and it remains to this day.'

Outside, I unpacked my picnic and left a little offering of food at the mouth of the cave – it seemed right to break bread with the saint's memory. As I munched my sandwich, I felt that this was the closest I'd yet come to him. I could have got there much more quickly by plane and train or car, but having earned the right to be there by putting in the miles and the days on the bike made it a much sweeter arrival. I took a few notes and pictures, then said goodbye.

A quick, sketchy descent down the muddy hairpins brought me back out to the main road, and a short spin to Annegray, a village that was not much more than a road sign. A grassy mound, perhaps half the size of a football pitch, sat beside a small chapel that looked suspiciously like a barn. An elderly man was up on the mound mowing the lawn. I nodded to him as I got off my bike, and entered the dark church, trying not to scrape the metal cleats on the soles of my shoes across the stone floor. Soon the gardener joined me to explain that indeed this had been a barn, but in the 1950s the local priest had campaigned to mark more satisfactorily the spot where Columbanus had founded his first monastery, and the barn had been converted. When Margaret Stokes was there, the site had been overgrown, and one of the medieval stone sarcophagi was being used as a drinking trough for cattle.

The chapel had a few modern paintings and statues of Columbanus, but it was the mound I really wanted to explore, and the gardener insisted on coming with me. He pointed out the foundations of the eleventh-century church, and the ring of raised ground that marks the original perimeter of the monastery. The rough circular enclosure in a prominent position reminded me of Monasterboice and, as helpful as the old man was being, I wanted to be there on my own. Every time I moved to take a picture, he was at my shoulder, watching intently, as if he'd never before seen such bizarre behaviour. Taking pictures? Walking around? These mad English. As I walked to another spot, he accompanied me, with another story of the visionary priest who had restored the site.

But it was a beautiful place, with a view down the valley towards the cave in the direction of Luxeuil. Behind, the higher peaks of the Jura were smudges of purple and grey. The valley floor today is largely given over to grazing, but it's easy to imagine it as the wooded expanse it must have been when Columbanus and his twelve followers arrived. It's still a remote place a long way from Ireland – how much more distant and remote must it have felt to the monks?

Back at the hotel, the day had changed. I switched on the television to the news of two passenger aircraft crashing into the World Trade Center in New York. I sat down on the bed and watched first one tower, then the other fold in on itself and slip away. From the distance of the cameras each collapse seemed as silent and effortless as a silk scarf falling off the back of a chair.

I'd been cruising around ancient sites of a religion I didn't even believe in while this horror was unfolding. I didn't know what I could have more usefully been doing, but congratulating myself on reaching the peaceful cave now seemed foolish and ignorant. I'd started writing in my notebook at exactly the time when the first plane had hit the towers.

On the radio, the BBC World Service knew no more than their TV colleagues, and without the constant repetition of the clips of the crashes, there wasn't much they could say. I showered and dressed, and for the next while wandered round the room swearing gently, then sitting down, getting up and forgetting what I was supposed to be doing. The scale of the violence was so huge that no one was mentioning casualties. New York and Washington were closed.

During my years in the States I'd visited New York City many times. Often I'd stayed at a friend's in Brooklyn while on my way from Kansas to Dublin, or I'd arrived for a few days when the prairies had made me long for hustle and people. I'd shopped for discount clothes at the foot of the Twin Towers, and used them as fixed points when navigating the streets up to Central Park. I'd turn a corner and look down one of the broad avenues to see the simple grey columns rising above the nearer rooftops.

Later I wandered down to the hotel restaurant for dinner, and was affronted that everything looked normal. At one table two middle-aged businessmen were discussing their starters, and at another sat an older German couple I recognised from breakfast. Richard Clayderman-style sub-classical meanderings were playing on the sound system as I ate my meal.

I went to sleep to news, and woke up to news. The details were getting more personal now – information on the fire-fighters who had rushed to the scene, and interviews with wives and mothers who had received desperate loving phone calls from men on the hijacked planes. There was still no word on the number of casualties. I had no desire to ride the bike. I sleep-walked through breakfast and packing up. Then, under appropriately leaden skies, I called in on Sonia at the tourist office to say goodbye.

I bought a paper at the newsagent's, and stopped outside to read my story. My old freelancer's eye appraised the layout and space given to the interview – lead story on a right-hand page, good-sized photo, not bad. Fabrice had tidied up my French, and now my answers made liberal use of the historic tense, which was interesting because I'd never been taught it. The first six pages of the newspaper were given to news of the previous day's attack. My very small story was sharing space with this massive event. A lot of articles would have been pulled to make room for the blanket coverage, and I was lucky to be in the paper at all, but that thought didn't help much.

On the way down to the post office, I bumped into Fabrice arriving to cover another story. At the post office I sent two big bundles of papers and maps home to Dublin, and as I was outside putting my gloves on, a young man stopped and wished me *'Bon courage, Monsieur.'* He must have seen the article. Four days before, I'd arrived here not knowing a soul, and now strangers were stopping me in the street. The celebrity was flattering, but I left Columbanus's town with a heavy heart – much as he had.

16

Through the Motions

Why, after twenty years, did Columbanus have to leave Luxeuil? For all his commitment to living the contemplative life, the saint was also immersed in politics, and it was his customary unwillingness to compromise that caused his downfall. While there might not seem to be many similarities between Dark Age ecclesiastical history and international football, Columbanus was the medieval precursor to Roy Keane. Both were uncompromising and principled to the point of self-destruction; both had problems when their commitment fo excellence was not shared by their colleagues, and both were sent home early. Columbanus would have approved of the Irish captain's response on being advised to go with the flow: 'Go with the flow? You know what goes with the flow? Dead fish.' If Columbanus had gone with the flow, he need never have left France.

It was a given of early medieval patronage that if you were granted land by the king to found a monastery, you offered spiritual support to the royal family. The monks would say prayers for them, and might also educate princes or other aristocratic children. In the early years of the monasteries in the Vosges, Columbanus had a good relationship with the young King Theuderic, who had assumed the throne in 596,

170

but his formidable grandmother Brunhilda wielded a great deal of power. She had been driven from the court of Theuderic's brother Theudebert, and seems to have been intent on securing her own power base with her other son.

The good terms didn't last. Jonas tells of Columbanus upbraiding Theuderic for living with concubines, and having children out of wedlock. The king agreed to mend his ways, but Brunhilda, 'a second Jezebel', feared that her own position would be threatened if Theuderic was to marry and bring a queen into the court. She invited Columbanus to one of the royal palaces and asked him to bless Theuderic's illegitimate children. Columbanus replied, 'Know that these boys will never bear the royal sceptre, for they were begotten in sin.'

This might sound like standard church doctrine, but even at the time some ecclesiastics argued that royal children were royal children, regardless of the marital status under which they were born. Columbanus's strict approach brought retaliation from Brunhilda, who forbade his monks to leave their lands and allowed no one to receive them into their houses. Columbanus visited Theuderic to argue his case. Except, being Columbanus, he arrived at the palace and refused to enter. The king sent food out to him but the saint rejected it, quoting the Bible: 'The Most High is not pleased with the offering of the wicked.' At these words the dishes shattered. I told you he was a hard-ass.

Columbanus was following the ancient Irish custom of fasting against someone in a dispute. In the sixth and seventh centuries in Ireland, public fasting overnight was the only way to compel a king to come to arbitration. To remain unmoved by the fast was to lose face. Theuderic might not have appreciated the cultural complexities of Columbanus's actions, but Jonas tells us that he and Brunhilda agreed to lift their sanctions against the monasteries.

However, the king was now almost as annoyed with the saint as his grandmother was, and they soon took up against him, with Brunhilda influencing the bishops 'to attack Columbanus's faith and to abolish his monastic rule'. In this they probably needed little prompting, as they had been critical of his conduct from the moment he arrived. The Irish Church, in which Columbanus had grown up, had no real diocesan structure and abbots were free to develop their own rules. This was the model that Columbanus had followed in France, bypassing the existing hierarchy of bishops.

His independence was seen most clearly in the date on which he celebrated Easter. This subject was the cause of great debate throughout early Christendom, with the Celtic Church adhering to a set of calculations that the Church in Rome had once used, not recognising a more recent ruling on the date.

Around 600, Columbanus had written to Pope Gregory the Great, respectfully telling him that he was wrong about Easter, and included a dig about the Frankish bishops – 'who ordain uncanonically, in other words, for hire … Gildas the writer set them down as simoniacs and plagues. Are we really to communicate with them?'

Seemingly not. In 603 Columbanus was summoned to a council of bishops in Chalon-sur-Saône, but he refused to go: if he went he'd only lose his temper and say the wrong thing. But he sent a letter asking 'that I may be allowed with your peace and charity to enjoy the silence of these woods and to live beside the bones of our seventeen dead brethren, even as now we have been allowed to live twelve years among you'.

Columbanus and the bishops reached an uneasy accommodation, but as the royal family were set against him he could expect little support from his fellow religious. When the king lost patience and had Columbanus arrested and taken to Besançon, none of the bishops objected. As we have seen, Columbanus escaped and returned to Luxeuil. When the troops arrived at the monastery a second time, there took place what newspapers would call a tense stand-off.

The soldiers told Columbanus that they were under orders to escort him out of Burgundy, and put him on a boat to Ireland. If he didn't come with them, they would risk death for failing in their duty. Initially the saint replied, 'I do not think it would be pleasing to my Creator that I should go back to the home which I left because of my love for Christ.' But the soldiers begged him, and Jonas tells us that he finally agreed to go so as not to put other people in danger. All his monks volunteered to go with him, but the king's men insisted that only Irishmen and Britons could leave with him. With much grief, the small band gathered their things and headed for the boat in Nantes that was supposed to take them back to Ireland. Of course, that didn't go exactly as the authorities planned, but Columbanus never saw Luxeuil again.

As I rolled out of town, I was pretty downcast too. Jonas mentions the sort of weather I was becoming used to in eastern France: 'The time had come for gathering the crops into the storehouses, but the violent winds did not cease to pile up clouds.' But today I hardly noticed the weather or the scenery. I wasn't in the mood for riding, but there wasn't anything else to do so I kept plodding along, with a bout of brain-fade in Melisey when I chose the wrong road out of town and had to double back a few kilometres. I was going through the motions, and not very convincingly.

Then it struck me that Columbanus was a religious extremist, a fundamentalist. His rigour was in many ways the same as that of the terrorists who had carried out the attacks on New York and Washington. His commitment to his faith was admirable, but it was also intolerant and inflexible. He forbade monks to talk, laugh or have any contact with their friends or family on pain of beating. He wanted his followers hungry and sleep-deprived and, crucially, he never entertained the possibility that he might be wrong. There's a telling moment in Jonas, when Columbanus is pondering whether he would prefer to 'suffer injuries from men, or to be exposed to the rage of wild beasts'. He decides that he'd choose the beasts because they would not be sinning if they attacked him. It's a bizarre enough question to ask yourself in the first place, but his conclusion is fascinating. The implication is that if men were injuring him, they *must* be in the wrong.

This view that other men must be sinners, when combined with the devaluing of life on earth in favour of an afterlife, can lead you to some cruel places, as the 11 September attackers had shown. I wasn't sure I liked my travelling companion very much any more. There was something to be said for the compromise, uncertainty and moderation that annoyed me about myself.

But cycling stops you being depressed. The absolute physicality of what you're doing draws your attention away from other thoughts and preoccupations. By the time I arrived in Belfort in the mid-afternoon I'd reached an accommodation with myself. There wasn't much point in what I was doing, especially when thousands of people had just died, but there'd be even less in stopping.

After Belfort the landscape opened up, with broader vistas and gentler hills. Villages bore German names and houses the timbered chalet look I'd last seen watching *Heidi* as a child. As I put up the tent at the campsite in Seppois, a German jazz radio station was playing songs about New York.

The next morning I headed off towards the border crossing at Basle. A teenage guard waved me through and that was it – I'd ridden my bike clear across France, from the western tip of Brittany to the Rhine. With no punctures.

Immediately things felt different. A tram line appeared, and after nearly a month of being surrounded by Peugeots, Renaults and Citroëns, here it was all VWs and Audis. I'd made a reservation at a hotel and soon my bike was safely stowed away and I was watching the latest news on the terrorist attacks in my starkly smart room.

I'd been in Basle once before, and had hated it so much I lied to the folks in the youth hostel so I could catch an overnight train to Milan rather than spend any more time there. I was Interrailing with a couple of schoolfriends in the summer before we all went to university, our heads full of notions of the Grand Tour. We'd had two glorious weeks in France before we arrived in Basle and instantly deemed it austerely Germanic, expensive and dull. None of us spoke the language and the whole city seemed a cultural backwater full of *bratwurst*-eating fools. We'd checked into the youth hostel beside the river, but as we walked around in the afternoon, we were so miserable that we planned our escape. To leave the hostel without staying the night would mean that we lost the money we'd already paid, so we concocted a story about an ill relative and I was nominated to wangle our money back.

I adopted a method-acting approach to my performance: I ran up and down the steps outside the hostel a few times so I'd be suitably flustered and out of breath when I made my entrance. Then I rushed through the spiel about how we had just called home to be told the bad news, and how we had to leave at once. I'm sure the bored guy behind the counter didn't care either way, but when he returned our money we felt like we'd cheated the system, and we headed for the railway station delighted with ourselves. Our overnight train took us across the Alps while we slept.

Parts of the centre of the city seemed familiar, but it was hard to work out why I'd disliked the place so vehemently last time. The picturesque streets were bustling, there were plenty of museums and galleries, and an air of confidence about the citizens. I found my way down to the river for my first view of the Rhine. Its broad green flow was constrained by high walls and, in addition to the bridges, a long narrow ferry punt toiled back and forth attached to a wire strung across the water.

I sat down outside a café for some coffee, still trying to get used to being in a different country. When you live on an island, venturing abroad takes a degree of effort, so simply riding a bike past a sign on the side of the road didn't seem to constitute an international journey.

Small candles were placed up the steps of a church on

Steinentorstrasse. A steady stream of people was going in, and near the altar a makeshift memorial had been erected to those who had died in New York and Washington. I added my candle to the full stands, and sat down near the front of the nave. Other people were scattered throughout the pews, driven to come to the church to pay their respects to the victims, but a little uncertain as to what to do now they were there. They were old and young, in suits and baggy combats, strangers joined in sympathy for people they had never known.

At the Internet café down the street, there were more immediate signs of the events in the US. A middle-aged American couple were checking their email to see if friends were stranded in unlikely cities – internal flights in the US were only just restarting. I read the *Irish Times* online: the next day was to be a day of mourning in Ireland. The Taoiseach Bertie Ahern expressed the hope that everyone would attend a religious service of their choosing. What if you didn't have a religion? Perhaps he just assumed that there were no atheists in the trenches. But religion seemed now to have a lot to answer for.

The Swiss eat earlier in the evening than the French, so it was a treat to be sitting in a busy restaurant at seven o'clock with so many people to watch. I was straining to overhear snippets of conversation and pick up some standard Swiss-German phrases that might be useful. '*Greuzi*' was 'hello', and the trilingually correct way to say 'no thanks, goodbye' was '*nein merci, ciao*'. Everyone spoke English, though, so I couldn't go too far wrong, and the diners in the restaurant looked like English people – slightly plumper and ruddier than the slim, nonchalantly stylish French. There was also a lot more beer than wine being drunk. Afterwards, I went for a nocturnal wander. Basle was buzzing – people were window-shopping, sitting outside cafés and bars, queuing for movies, and there were bikes everywhere. Young women in party clothes were riding sturdy city bikes with dynamo lights and kickstands, and the people who weren't walking or cycling were getting on and off spotless green trams. Dublin's planners would have wept at the sight.

In Barfüsserplatz market stalls were set up in front of the museum, selling jewellery, funky clothes and food. I stood on the steps and surveyed the busy square – trams, bikes, kite stalls, steep Swiss buildings, the smell of bread and cakes in the air, and the hum of happy conversation. It was great, and I was glad to be there to see it. How could I have been so wrong about this place when I was there all those years ago? Bloody students, they don't know anything.

17

A Day in the Life

At home, I'm lucky if I do one memorable thing a week, and I couldn't tell you what I had for lunch yesterday, but some travelling days stand out, large and brightly coloured in my memory, like my first full day in Switzerland.

Leaving Basle, I was accompanied by polite articulated lorries as I rode past the industrial complexes that contribute to the high Swiss standard of living. It wasn't pretty, but the roads were good, and I managed a detour to Augusta Rurica – a Roman settlement that was being carefully restored. I dodged the school parties and had a quick look at the red-brick amphitheatre, but the real success of the visit was in connecting with one of the nine national cycling routes.

Once I had spotted a red triangular sign with a bike in it, I was off on a magical mystery tour for big chunks of the day. The cycle routes lead you in car-free comfort through lumber yards, behind factories, across fields and beside nuclear power stations on their way between towns. The closest you come to traffic is when the kids get out of school, and the kilometres had come easily as I arrived in Rheinfelden.

I'd never been to Germany so, seizing my chance, I rode over the picturesque cobbled bridge across the Rhine and was again waved through the customs post (note to prospective drug traffickers: it seems security is extremely lax if you're on a bike, and you could squeeze a lot of gear into two Ortlieb panniers). Notching up another country was cool, but this wasn't the direction I was supposed to be travelling in, so I turned round about fifty yards past the border, and rode back over the bridge.

The bike paths are great because they take you off the roads, but this has its drawbacks. As a devoted map-head, I'd spent a month being sure of exactly where I was at almost every moment. My map of the cycle routes was vague so when I arrived at junctions I had to rely on the little red triangles.

It was fine until the Tarmac turned into a muddy footpath on the other side of Rheinfelden. I guessed the smooth stuff would soon reappear, so I prepared myself for a brief spell of offroading. The heavy bike was surprisingly stable as it bounced over half-buried rocks and gouged out a line through the light brown clay. I like mountain-biking, and have fallen off expensive bikes into bushes on three continents. I've also mastered a range of mountain-bike vocabulary, distinguishing between 'baby heads' (large, loose rocks around the size of, well, babies' heads) and 'death cookies' (smaller flatter stones that tend to take your front wheel away from you). I knew that gnarly riders rode double-bangers made of unobtainium, while novices had chain-ring tattoos and ended up doing horizontal track-stands when they couldn't clip out of their spuddies. I was down with the baggier and less colourful (but no less technical) clothing worn by MTBers, who are to road-racing cyclists as funky snowboarders are to skiers. I'd been known to catch some big air, and had once caught some spectacular 'Jesus Christ air' – immediately before my most spectacular crash.

Mountain-biking is great, but you need to be on a mountain bike to do it, and the Tarmac was showing no sign of imminent return. I could hear rattles from places on the touring bike that definitely shouldn't have been rattling. The panniers were making a concerted effort to jump off the rack, and my mud-covered trip computer told me I was riding at a feeble twelve kilometres an hour. The delightful absence of cars didn't seem so delightful now that the bike was shaking itself to bits over tree roots. Normally you go out mountain-biking for a few hours on a bike designed to take a ridiculous amount of abuse, knowing that you'll soon be home again, where you can true the wheels and pull the derailleur out of the rear spokes. This time I had to get my bike over the Alps to Italy. I should have been looking after it.

Finally I found a road, and continued my journey running parallel to the Rhine. The river was as wide as the Loire had been, but its turbid flow was much faster. Germany was on the other side, and I still couldn't get used to that, but I made good time, and arrived outside the small town of Koblenz in mid-afternoon to see where the river Limmat met the Rhine.

When Columbanus escaped being sent back to Ireland by making his vessel run aground outside Nantes, he turned inland and travelled all the way back across France. Journeying north, to avoid Theuderic's kingdom, he was welcomed by King Chlotar, and given guides to take him eastwards to the kingdom of Austrasia ruled by Theuderic's brother (and enemy) Theudebert. According to Jonas, Columbanus had told Chlotar that he wished to travel to Italy, and the saint himself had written to Pope Gregory the Great as early as 600 saying that he longed to visit Rome. Columbanus's fame preceded him, and Theudebert treated him most hospitably at his court in Metz in what is now north-eastern France. Of course, there was a political angle to the welcome: the king was keen to be associated with an abbot whose prestige was only matched by his opposition to his brother. The enemy of my enemy…

Columbanus was joined there by some of his monks who had come from Luxeuil to see him. Jonas says that 'the king promised to seek out beautiful places, suitable for God's servants, where they could preach to the neighbouring people.' The saint seemed willing to delay his planned journey to Italy to help in this missionary work, and chose a 'long-ruined city' as his base – Brigantia (now Bregenz) on Lake Constance. It was easily reached along the Rhine, and stood at the foot of an old Roman road over the Alps, so perhaps this was a convenient compromise: Theudebert got to enjoy the prestige and practical benefits of having Columbanus found a monastery in his kingdom while Columbanus would be helped on his journey to Italy if he decided to move on.

The saint and his party journeyed to Mainz, where they boarded boats for the trip on the Rhine. They would have passed through Basle and continued eastwards, but when they reached Koblenz, where I'd now arrived, they had a choice. There the Rhine is joined by the Limmat, but at the meeting of the waters it's unclear which is the major flow. Jonas is quiet on much of the monks' Swiss journeying, but Walahfrid Strabo, author of the *Life of St Gall*, one of

Columbanus's companions, filled in some of the details. It seems the monks took a wrong turning in their boat, rowing up the Limmat and into Lake Zurich rather than bearing left and following the Rhine into Lake Constance.

As I stood on the bridge at the spot where the two rivers join, it was easy to see how you could choose the wrong river: the Limmat looks bigger at that point. For me, as for the monks, the easiest way to get to Bregenz would have been to stay alongside the Rhine, but since I'd skipped their river journeys further north (Metz and Mainz were a long way out of my way), I felt I should get back into following Columbanus more closely, so I took the same wrong turn as they had and followed the Limmat towards Baden, a few kilometres north of Zurich.

The intermittent showers I'd been facing all day finally abated, and as the sun came out it warmed the roads so quickly they started to steam. I rode partly on empty ones, partly on the cycle paths, and discovered how important bicycles are to everyday Swiss life. Outside apartment blocks there were rows of sheltered bike-stands. The national cycle route I was riding along was crossed by lots of local paths connecting towns and villages, providing a safe, well-signposted alternative to taking your car. In France people had been enthusiastic about bikes without creating a dedicated infrastructure for them, but in Switzerland bikes were a priority.

With one final slog out of a steep-sided valley, I arrived in Baden. The woman in the tourist office told me that while there was a campsite I'd be better off at the youth hostel. 'It is not like the campsites in the mountains … and the youth hostel is very nice,' she said carefully.

I wheeled the bike through the pedestrianised old town and out to a modern bridge that spanned the river valley. It was a long way down to the river, and the town's castle was behind me on a steep wooded hill. I crossed the bridge and found my way to the campsite, down a steep, winding lane. I immediately saw what the tourist-office woman had meant. The site was smaller than a football pitch, and tents and caravans were strewn across it randomly. There was no privacy, and everything looked dirty and unkempt. Half a dozen empty beer bottles were lined up outside one of the tents. In the far corner from the entrance there was a wooden shack, not much more than a roof over a table. No one was around.

I walked over to the rubbish-strewn shack, but had already decided I wasn't going to stay there. Amid the pile of old magazines and dirty dishes that sat on the table was a sign that said the proprietor would be back at six o'clock. It was now five forty-five, and I wanted to escape before anyone arrived and made me stay in this home for Swiss derelicts. Time for plan B – the youth hostel.

It was a smart two-storey building. Inside, the grey stone floor led to a reception desk made of blond wood. It reminded me of a new block on a university campus – bright and airy, with signs written in a lower-case sans-serif typeface. The man who booked me in looked at my Irish youth-hostel-association card and laughed. 'Always there are you Irish people here. Some left today.'

'Well, we get everywhere.'

'I know some Gaelic.'

'Really?' It was more than I did.

'*Póg mo thóin.* That's right, yes?'

Ah, the one bit of Irish I and most other Anglophone people do know – 'kiss my arse'.

'The good thing of working in a youth hostel: I can swear in many languages.'

Along with the sheet, duvet cover and pillowcases, I was given a high-tech key card for my door – hostels had moved on since I'd last been in one. My room had three sets of bunk beds and three young guys in it. One was asleep on a top bunk, the other two were lying down reading computer magazines. A radio was playing, and they looked like they'd been there for a while – washing was draped over the radiator, someone's shoes were on the ledge outside the window, and toiletries and bottles of water stood on the small table. I said hello to the room in general, and was met with a couple of grunts and nods.

It was clear that they all knew one another, and I felt like I'd arrived at a stranger's house and told them I'd be staying for the night. But this was a lot better than the dodgy campsite, so I stowed my stuff in the wooden lockers inside the door and went for a shower.

Back at the room, one of the guys was retrieving his shoes from the window-ledge as it had started to rain hard – another reason to be grateful for the roof over my head. The three of them were getting ready to go out, and one asked me in English where I was from. I told him, and explained a little about my trip. 'So, are you travelling yourself?' I asked.

'No, I move here for a job,' he said. 'The company gives me an apartment, but it is not ready yet. So I wait here.'

'How long have you been here?'

'Three weeks. I go to my home at weekends. It is not so bad.'

It didn't seem great to me – starting a new job and having to live in a youth hostel. They pulled on their coats and left the room – it was Friday night, and the working lads were off out on the batter in Baden.

I was soon back in town too. On the way to dinner, a young man in a suit came up to me and started asking for directions. I fumbled towards the small bit of German I knew: '*Ich bin auslander.*'

'Ah, I'm sorry,' he said in English. 'I thought you lived here.'

It wasn't the first time I'd been mistaken for a local. In Angers I'd been walking back to the corporate hotel after my meal when a guy in an old Renault 5 pulled up beside me looking for directions. The same thing had happened in Tours and Auxerre. As I sipped a giant glass of wheat beer in a bar after dinner, I wondered if being taken for a local was such a good thing. The other men in the place were all sporting classic 1980s German footballer haircuts. I hadn't seen so many mullets since I'd left Kansas, or as many moustaches since I'd left San Francisco. One guy was even wearing marble-washed jeans. The few women in the place seemed a little less anachronistic, but I sensed I was in a town that was happy with itself, and didn't much care what was happening in the rest of the world. Which was fine, of course, except that I obviously looked like I fitted right in.

Back at the hostel, I gathered some maps and sat in the dining room to plan where I was going after Zurich. I'd just got settled when I was joined by the wife of the man who had checked me in. She was Israeli, and obviously found it hard to keep up with her husband's proficiency in languages. Every so often, she'd forget she'd been speaking English, and continue in German. Sometimes I'd correct her, but mostly I just nodded.

She and her husband had been running hostels for years, partly so they could go and stay at others for free. They'd toured Ireland in an old VW bus, and she'd liked it but couldn't remember any of the places they'd been. She asked me where I was travelling to, and when I told her, she looked at me as though I was insane. 'From Brittany? Not all the way on bicycle?'

'Yep, two thousand kilometres,' I said. It was the first time I'd tried this big number on anyone. I'd clocked up the 2K on the way out of Basle the previous day, and had stopped on the bike path to take a picture of the distance on my computer – an interesting variation on the road-sign theme.

'But you sometimes put the bicycle on the train, no?'

'No. I've ridden every last metre from Dublin. Except the ferry, of course.'

'But the traffic, in the cities. I ride, but I go on the paths, you know, for bicycles? Is dangerous on the road.'

'It's a lot safer here than in Ireland. I'm used to it.'

'You go to Italy?' She leaned forward over my map.

'I think I'm going over the Splugen Pass. Up through Chur, and then down to Lake Como.' I traced the route with my finger, pronouncing 'Chur' like 'churlish'.

She paused for a while, and then let out the sound of a projectile vomit – 'Huuuuugggghrr!' Cycling might not be her cup of tea, but this was a bit harsh.

She pointed at the map, and let out the same noise. 'Huuuuugggghrr. It's pronounced Huuuuugggghrr, not Chur,' she said. 'But you don't go over the mountains. They are very high. Snow. Difficult to drive, but with bike? Is impossible.'

She sounded like a Jewish Yoda and I didn't believe her but, then, I'd never seen the Alps. 'I'll be all right. I've ridden in the Rockies in America, and they're higher than the pass I'm going over. I'm sure I'll be fine.'

She didn't look convinced, and pointed towards Bregenz and Lake Constance. 'You go here, and then you go home. No mountains, understand?'

'I'll be fine,' I repeated, a little less sure now.

18

Undercapitalised and Climbing

The menu was in Italian and German, and having next to no German I'd ordered in Italian, so now the German-speaking Swiss waitress thought that her Anglo-Irish diner was from Bergamo not Buckinghamshire. Such is life in confident cosmopolitan Zurich, where I'd spent a pleasant Saturday. I'd wandered around the smart shops in the centre of town, and ambled down to the lake shore where the water draws your gaze out to the silver horizon.

Zurich is a city that's literally built on money – you walk over bank vaults as you window-shop your way down Bahnhofstrasse. Even the dodgy sex clubs near my hotel looked smart. Interior-design shops vied with upscale clothes outlets to attract the attention of well-dressed locals, and late-model Mercedes and Audi estates purred down the clean wide streets. Even the bikes people were riding were expensively over-engineered for urban commuting. I saw a guy in a suit pedalling over one of the bridges on a Cannondale mountain bike worth around two thousand euros. He was using it like it was a Raleigh shopper – I was both underdressed and undercapitalised.

And underslept. The previous night I'd retired to my top bunk in the design-led hostel while my roommates were out doing whatever young men do in Baden. I was sound asleep, dreaming of endless downhills and sunny weather, when they tumbled drunk through the door. Joking in loud stage-whispers, they switched on the light over the washbasin in the corner, rather than the one overhead. Fair play to them, I thought – at least they're trying to be considerate. Then they switched on the radio, and started singing along to Britney Spears: 'Hit Me, Baby, One More Time'. I couldn't believe it. Somebody certainly deserved a good slap.

Fortunately, the ride into Zurich was short and straight-forward and I was soon established in my 1970s pimp-chic hotel room. The walls and floor of the bathroom were covered with tiny dark blue tiles, and a glass cabinet offered a selection of toiletries for the forgetful guest who didn't mind paying for his mistakes. The men's products were from Tabac – their brown packaging hadn't changed since it was my father's Christmas favourite when Brotherhood of Man were bossing the charts. The bed had a complicated headboard-cum-bedside-table thing, which boasted a built-in radio with a row of black buttons for channel selection. Groovy.

Columbanus took a lot of boats, and since the ferry crossing from Ireland I'd not taken any, but Sunday morning saw me down at the landing stage for the steamers that go back and forth across Lake Zurich. It must have been an amazing experience for the saint and his followers to travel down the river and out into the expanse of the lake, even if it wasn't the one they were looking for. Their wrong turn in Koblenz had left them in territory that was largely pagan, but it's unclear if they knew they were lost. They sailed across the wrong lake and landed near the end on the right-hand side, arriving at the village of Tuggen, which was my next target.

It was grey and cold again, and on the boat the patchy rain drove everyone inside. The boat crossed and recrossed the narrow lake, stopping at small towns whose names were painted in bright letters on the jetties. The mountains were shrouded in cloud, but as we chugged along, I eyed up a large number of desirable lake-shore properties nestling among the pine trees.

The bike and I got off in Rapperswill and I dropped into the tourist office to check on campsites further up the road. There weren't any, and the woman told me cheerfully that the forecast was for rain and more rain. Down the road, the village of Tuggen lay in a broad flat valley, just back from the water. According to Walahfrid Strabo, when Columbanus and his followers arrived there it 'appeared to them well-fitted for a settlement'.

They began to get themselves settled, but one of the monks, Gall, was as uncompromising as his abbot when it came to the expression of his faith. He was one of the original twelve who had set sail from Bangor all those years previously, and he seems to have found it particularly difficult to be surrounded by pagans. In Luxeuil, they might have been out in the wilds but they were teaching the children of the aristocracy, and were afforded the luxury of doctrinal disputes with the local bishops. Here things were different. Strabo gives us an unflattering portrait of the resident Alemmanians, who had arrived in these high valleys in the fifth century – they were 'cruel and irreligious, given to image-worship and sacrifices in honour of idols, and practising augury and divination and many other superstitious customs contrary to the worship of God'.

Gall had a simple solution to their image-worshipping. He collected up as many of their images as he could find and dumped them in the lake. Then, to underline his brand of hardcore Christianity, he set fire to their temples. The Alemmanians were not impressed by this and retaliated by trying to kill him. Columbanus got the message, so they gathered up their things and headed off again – this time up into the hills.

This was the part of the story I wasn't so keen on – the uphill bit. I'd ridden up a few steep climbs in the month I'd been away, but nothing that could have been called a mountain. My conversation in the hostel in Baden had worried me a little, and now I'd find out if I'd brought my climbing legs with me. Tuggen had calmed down since Gall adopted his zero-tolerance policy – it was now a sleepy damp town with lots of space between the large houses. When the rain cleared for a time, I looked to the south and saw a set of peaks higher than those that ringed the lake and topped with snow. Nobody had told me there'd be snow.

Columbanus seems to have asked directions as he and his monks legged it from Tuggen. They had been told of a larger lake to the north-west – Lake Constance, with Bregenz on its eastern shore, where they were supposed to have been in the first place. I was following them, so for the moment I could turn my back on the really big mountains and focus on getting over the moderately high peaks that lay in the other direction. I spun round the end of the lake with growing trepidation, then started going uphill in earnest.

Some bikes are light, twitchy machines that accelerate the

moment you get out of the saddle, and come alive on hills. All your power is transferred instantly to the back wheel, and you go out of your way to find hills because going up them is such fun. I realised I'd reached a watershed in my cycling career one Sunday in San Francisco. I was riding my normal route over the Golden Gate Bridge and into the hills on the north side. Immediately over the bridge there is a turn-off to a steep climb that winds round the front of the headlands, so you climb with a view of the city and the ocean to your left. I'd made it up the hill in good shape, enjoying the eagerness of my new light racing bike. I didn't want to be out too long, so I carved my way down to the bottom of the hill again. When I got there, I realised it had been more fun on the way up than on the way down – a timid descender, I preferred pushing myself to the limit in terms of physical stamina rather than risk-taking. This was bad enough, but I was unprepared for what happened next. I turned the bike round, and attacked the bottom of the climb again, dancing on the pedals of my sleek titanium steed. Some bikes like climbing so much, they even make *you* like it.

But now I was on a heavy old touring bike, climbing like an eighteen-wheeler in a crawler lane. With the panniers on the back and the handlebar-bag on the front it was very hard to get out of the saddle and throw the thing around. I could only honk when not to do so would result in me coming to a standstill and falling off sideways. It was no fun to ride, but it did have a large number of easy gears, which meant I could sit and spin no matter how slowly I was going.

So up and around the first few hairpins I rode, finding a slow but comfortable rhythm. If you'd been walking energetically up the hill, I wouldn't have caught you, but once I found my groove I didn't care. After twenty minutes I was about two-thirds of the way up, and the rain was coming down steadily, so I adjourned for lunch in the shelter of a petrol-station forecourt. It might not be the stuff of many Alpine adventures, but it was dry. A squad of vintage Spitfires and MGs slooshed past me on the way up, and this gave me heart to continue. If the sensible Swiss were trusting themselves to the antique British electrical systems in those cars, I reckoned I could make it to the top.

I was cold and wet, but eventually I reached the tiny village of Ricken at the top of the pass. I'd half planned to stay there, as I didn't like the idea of a sketchy descent in the rain with my feeble brakes. But, flushed with success from the climb, I accelerated through the village and made for Wattwil, seven kilometres away, and all downhill. The road surface was good, but there was quite a lot of traffic so I tucked myself into the side of the road and tried to scrub off as much speed as I could as I approached the corners. Then the road straightened out and dropped more steeply; the spray was flying everywhere, I couldn't see much, and the heavy bike was gaining speed rapidly, but it still felt steady, so I held it straight and let it go.

Ahead was a road sign, but I couldn't see it clearly until I was almost on top of it. It showed a junction ahead, with a sharp right turn for Wattwil. I was doing over fifty k.p.h. when I saw a set of traffic lights immediately ahead. It was the junction, and the lights were red. I slammed on the brakes, but they couldn't grip on the dripping rims. I pulled harder, white-knuckling the levers almost into the handle-bars, and finally started slowing. Not enough to stop at the junction, however, so I turned right and veered into the middle of the slip road. Fortunately no one was coming the other way, and I pulled the bike back into line as the road levelled off. Made it.

I found a modern hotel that had a bar and restaurant in the main building, and two storeys of rooms in an extension to one side. The elderly woman running the place only spoke German, but with a friendly exchange of sign-language we got everything squared away – the bike ended up in a garage to dry out, and I was soon drying out in another 1970s hotel room. This one had brown carpets and a bathroom with cream tiles and an orange toilet and sink. But there was plenty of hot water and BBC Prime on the television, so after my shower I did my stretches while watching an episode of *Grange Hill*. It was a bizarre thing to be watching in a Swiss village, and I imagined the locals arguing over whether or not the early episodes with Zammo and Tucker Jenkins were better than the current series.

The woman at the tourist office in Rapperswill had been right. It was raining hard, and had been all night. The forecast was for more rain all day today, and I was nervous as I sat in the hotel restaurant eating bread and cheese – breakfast had come over all Germanic since Basle. The top of the hill I'd come down yesterday was obscured with cloud. The expensive cars were driving by with full headlights on, even though it was nearly nine o'clock. A guy cycled past holding a brolly in one hand – a nice trick, but it wasn't going to help me any as I hadn't brought mine with me. I had two mountain passes to get over in the forty kilometres to St Gallen, my destination for the day. Both were higher than the one I'd crossed yesterday, and the rain showed no sign of abating. I was anxious about the getting up – this was more climbing than I'd ever done on the touring bike – and equally so about the getting down: in the rain, my brake blocks were like bars of soap.

I checked and rechecked the maps, and lingered over my coffee, but sooner rather than later I'd have to get out in it and see what happened. I wasn't going to stay there, I wasn't going to cheat by getting a lift over the passes, and if I waited to see what the weather did, it might get worse rather than better. It was time to suck it up. I said goodbye to the landlady, and retrieved the bike from the garage. I was wearing my full complement of layers – cycling jersey with the long sleeves added, fleece top with the zip done all the way up, and the waterproof jacket that was only proving partially waterproof (which is like being a little bit pregnant). I had my long leg-warmers on, and two pairs of socks inside my shoes, which had dried out overnight next to the radiator.

I rode along the valley for the first few kilometres, but as I started on the first climb the rain eased off and my mood improved. The hairpins were steep, and as you looked up approaching the corner you could see cars coming down to meet you at ridiculous angles. With a few hairpins completed, I looked down to the roofs of the village I'd just ridden through. Banks of cloud were draped around the pine trees at the top of the mountains, but down in the valleys the grass was bright green and smooth as baize.

The altimeter on my giant watch told me I was at 850 metres (around 2800 feet) – not that high, but I was happy with the achievement as I dropped my hands into the crooks of the handlebars for the descent. I sped through St

Peterzell, and on to the next pass. This time the road was straight, and it was a long, easy pull up to 905 metres. I was loving this. The weather had improved, and the bike and I seemed in great shape. I laughed to myself as I rode along. There was a lot of snow not far above me, but the road was clear and in excellent condition. There was even a cycle lane for parts of the ride, and half a dozen red-faced school-children aged about eleven pedalled past me in the opposite direction. I dropped down and down to Herisau as the clouds closed in again. Police and ambulance sirens cut into my good spirits, and I slowed as I encountered my first traffic of the day. A policeman was waving the cars past the remains of a motor scooter, which were strewn all over the greasy road. I shuddered as I passed, and with the rain starting in earnest, I joined the main road to St Gallen for the final flat spin into town.

19

Homesick Felt Slippers

I was taking liberties with Columbanus's route again. When his party had left Tuggen, they'd gone straight over the mountains to the north-east, stopping at Arbon, a small settlement on the shores of Lake Constance, on their way to Bregenz. St Gallen didn't even exist when they'd passed this way, but its history owes much to Columbanus's party – it was founded by Columbanus's temple-burning companion Gall. I had to pay it a visit, even if it was a little out of sequence.

Gall got to found St Gallen because he said he was too ill to travel when the monks moved on from Bregenz, now making for Italy. Columbanus, showing a marked lack of Christian compassion, thought that 'Gall was held back by love of a spot endeared to him by many labours and was shirking the fatigue of a long journey', as Walahfrid Strabo tells the story. Columbanus forbade him to celebrate mass as long as he, Columbanus, lived. With that, he left one of his oldest friends beside the lake, and headed off over the mountains. He really *was* like Roy Keane: extremely loyal, leading by example and sheer force of will. However, the commitment and bloody-mindedness required to achieve great things also has a downside: the inability to accept what appears to be less than total commitment from others. If Gall was not going to support his master on this, then all the other times he had supported him counted for nothing. Gall had shown disloyalty, and Columbanus had no time for those who were disloyal.

We'll never know if Gall really was ill, and he outlived Columbanus, which suggests at least that he recovered from his ailment. We're also told that during the monks' time in Switzerland it was Gall who was best at learning the local languages, so perhaps he felt settled and didn't want to embark on another trying journey. Left alone, he looked for a remote retreat, and found 'a wild and fearsome place, full of high mountains with narrow winding glens and haunted by savage beasts'. It was a day's walk from the lake shore, and when he found the spot, he rested beside a river where it formed a pool beside a cliff. He caught some fish, and as he was cooking them over a fire, a bear emerged from the gathering gloom. Gall obviously shared Columbanus's touch with wild animals, because he told the bear to make himself useful and throw another log on the fire. The bear did as instructed, and later Gall built a small church on the spot, with some cells for fellow brethren. In this way he founded the monastery and town that are named for him – St Gallen.

Despite his outburst beside Lake Zurich, Gall seems to have been a little calmer and more human than Columbanus. I imagine him initially hurt and shocked at the way he was abandoned, but later coming to relish his quiet independence away from the brilliant but difficult Columbanus. He seems to have had little ambition – he was offered the see of Constance, and the chance to return to Luxeuil as abbot, but preferred to stay in the mountains. The monastery he founded went on to become a crucial centre for learning in the eighth and ninth centuries and to this day its library still contains more than half of the manuscripts written by Irishmen in those years.

With all this in mind, I was expecting St Gallen still to have some traces of retreat and reflection, but it's a busy city with Gall's original church buried under a huge baroque cathedral longer than a football pitch. Even though I was still over 650 metres high, I couldn't see the mountains from anywhere in the centre of town.

I was continuing my tour of Swiss time-warp accommodation. My room above a bar boasted 1960s net curtains, cold parquet flooring and a sink in the corner. But it was cheap, and on the wall outside a sign showed a bear bringing a monk an oversized sheaf of wheat. The monk looks as if he's checking it in the interests of holy quality control, and the one-word inscription beneath it told me I was definitely in the right place: *GALLUSBRAU*. There was even a beer named for Gall. If he could get his friendly bear to bring him firewood, maybe he also trained him up as a master-brewer. Gall himself would certainly have had some experience of the craft, as it was the one luxury the monks were allowed in Luxeuil. Columbanus's Italian biographer Jonas was most confused over the frothy stuff, 'which is boiled down from the juice of corn or barley, and which is used in preference to other beverages by the barbarous nations that inhabit the ocean, that is, in Gaul, Britain, Ireland, Germany'. A contemporary account of an exchange between two Irish abbots shows there was some difference of opinion at home on the subject. 'The drink of forgetfulness of God shall not be drunk here,' said the abbot of Tallaght. 'Well, my household shall drink it,' replied the abbot of Finglas, 'and they will be in heaven along with your household.' I'll have a pint of the-drink-of-forgetfulness-of-God, when you're ready, please, barman.

As I was leaving the guesthouse, the landlady gestured to me that it was raining.

'I know,' I said, shrugging. My cycling jacket didn't have a hood, because the designers had presumed you'd be wearing a helmet.

She acted out opening an umbrella. I shook my head. She'd seen me arrive on the bike – where did she think I'd put the brolly?

She looked annoyed with me. I was glad she didn't speak English, because I'd say she was about to tell me exactly what she thought of people who came unprepared to her rainy town. I turned towards the door. 'Please,' she said, motioning that I should wait. She disappeared into the kitchen and came back with a black telescopic umbrella. She looked like she was going to clip me round the ear with it, so I'd remember for next time. But then she handed it over with what passed for a smile.

I made straight for the cathedral, which lies on one side of a large grass quadrangle, with red-tiled municipal buildings making up the other sides. Inside, the sturdy white pillars seemed to be straining to support the weight of the ornately painted ceiling, and the tall windows let in a clear, natural light. I had a cursory glance round for some monument to Gall among all the overweight cherubim sitting on cotton-wool clouds, but couldn't find anything. After the Gothic splendours I'd seen in France, it all felt overblown, but the scale of the place is impressive.

Aside from the cathedral, there were two styles of architecture on view in St Gallen. One was the traditional timber-framed house with a sharp roof and oriel windows, and the other was the austere concrete box with sad-looking stains from the rain on the bare external walls. Somehow both styles worked well side by side, and I ducked into one of the concrete boxes to check my email. Two teenage girls, dressed beyond their years, were at the computer next to me. A Prada bag hung over the back of one of the chairs, and its owner was reading an email aloud to her friend in English. Her accent had a slight American veneer on top of the Germanic vowels, as if she'd spent too long watching *Dawson's Creek*. It was from an ex-boyfriend, who sounded American: 'I really value the time we had together, and now I realise just how awesome you are. When I think of all the wonderful and rewarding experiences you gave me, I can't believe that we're not still together.'

Prada Girl snorted and let out a short guttural sentence in what I took to be German, but could have been Klingon, it was so full of venomous contempt for the luckless dude. I didn't rate his chances for a reconciliation.

That night I ate *rösti* – one of a limited number of Swiss contributions to world cuisine. (I know fondue is Swiss too, but this isn't the 1970s any more – except in guesthouses and hotels all over the country.) *Rösti* are wedges of roast potato served with melted cheese and a range of other toppings. I chose the vegetarian option, but my dinner looked as if it was waiting for a big slab of meat to go with it. All my years in Ireland should have made me the perfect candidate for a plateful of spuds, but I wasn't impressed. Cycling had turned me into a carnivore.

*

The St Gallen library continued the baroque style of the cathedral. At the end of a long corridor you're given felt slippers to put over your shoes before entering the library. I wanted to take a big run-up and slide along the highly polished floor, but I tried to disconnect the juvenile part of my brain and pay attention. Ornate bookcases alternated with full-length windows in the high-ceilinged room. Above was a gently concave ceiling with massive frescoes framed by swirling white plasterwork. This cathedral of books is a staggering sight, and I felt sheepish as I stood in the doorway wearing a pair of grey slippers and a crinkly waterproof.

Two rows of display cabinets stretched the length of the room, and I joined the heavy German tourists poring over the priceless codices within. Irish monks travelled to St Gallen and its sister foundations throughout the early medieval period, and the beauty of the books they produced has scarcely been equalled. In one of the cases was the famous St Gall Gospel, written in Ireland shortly after 750 in a graceful round half-uncial hand; in the next was the glorious Long Gospel from the Carolingian Renaissance, with an ivory cover made by a St Gallen monk around 894. Next up came the Golden Psalter, written in ink made from gold at the palace school of Charles the Bald in Soissons around 860 and completed in St Gallen between 870 and 900. Writing each of these manuscripts was a massive undertaking requiring years of consummate talent and discipline. They were the skyscrapers of their time, standing proud above the mundanities of daily life. We now know how vulnerable real skyscrapers can be, so it's even more amazing that these delicate objects have lasted millennia –

the next case contained the earliest surviving catalogue of the St Gallen library, dating from around 880. Two-thirds of the manuscripts are still there today.

Each codex seemed to float in its glass case with an aura of the miraculous. Gerald of Wales, a twelfth-century traveller to Ireland, was no Hibernophile, but on being shown an early Irish illuminated Gospel he was moved to comment, 'If you take the trouble to look very closely, and penetrate with your eyes to the secrets of the artistry, you notice such intricacies, so delicate and subtle, so close together and well-knitted, so involved and bound together, and so fresh still in their colourings that you will not hesitate to declare that all these things must have been the work, not of men, but of angels.'

It was hard to associate the shining manuscripts with the grim, dirty lives led by Columbanus and his followers – the founders of the monasteries where much of this work took place. From Jonas's *Life* and his own writings, it seems that scholarship was less of a priority for Columbanus than mortification, obedience and trying to avoid starving to death. Despite his own deep learning and the twenty years he was in France, we have no manuscripts from his time in Luxeuil, and the first we have from there are written in a distinctly non-Irish hand. It was for later Irishmen travelling across Europe to bring their unique vision of what the word of God should look like on the page – the Lord made text.

My introduction to these wonderful objects came in Cambridge. Palaeography (the study of manuscripts) was, to my geeky mind, a surprisingly sexy subject, and I imagined myself as a cross between Indiana Jones and Sherlock Holmes. The adventurous part came in being so close to priceless artefacts from over a millennium ago. The vellum showed the traces of veins from the cows that had died to offer up their skins as a writing surface. There were rules scored into the page so the lines were straight, and little spots of ink where the quill nib had skidded or split. Examining them was a form of time travel. In truth, most of the material we handled was photocopied in the departmental office half an hour before class, but we were encouraged to go into the Manuscripts Room in the university library and call up some of their fabulous holdings to see the stuff for real. It was easy to pretend the pages had fallen out of an old book in a draughty country-house library, unseen for centuries until you discovered them.

The Sherlock Holmes part of the work came from the incredible amount of information it was possible to deduce from a careful study of the script. Writing styles differed across regions and centuries, and the differences showed in the way letter shapes were formed, the abbreviations used, and other minor details. If you knew your stuff, you could date and place manuscripts to within a decade, and even identify individual scribes by their flourishes or mistakes: 'This is clearly Northumbrian half-uncial phase two, from early 785. The finials on the "g" and the use of the mannered ampersand and "fl" ligatures suggest it was written in the south-facing windows of the scriptorium in Monkwear-mouth on a wet Tuesday afternoon by a monk with a runny nose.' Or something like that.

I was staying another night in St Gallen – the last day off the bike before I started towards the Alps – so I had plenty of time to walk the streets, drink the coffee and get a feel for the town. One obvious thing was the number of quietly expensive cars parked around the place. For someone with four bikes and no car, I spent a lot of time thinking about these metal boxes. Many of the St Gallen cars were limited edition or customised new Audis, VWs and BMWs. Instead of ostentatious spoilers or go-faster stripes, there were discreet M3 or Sporting Audi badges, and even a few with no badges at all – mute testament to some tricky after-market tweaking: here a stiffened suspension, there a re-chipped and balanced engine twinned with chunkier brake discs and callipers. By the time I'd seen my second V6 four-wheel-drive Golf of the afternoon, I'd resolved that, despite my fear of offices, I'd return to Dublin and pimp my soul for a cool set of wheels.

Thinking a movie might take my mind off this nonsense, I checked what was playing at the cinemas in town. And what language it was playing in. There were films in German, French, Italian and English. I couldn't work out if the German ones came with French subtitles and vice versa, or whether the English ones came with subtitles in all the Swiss languages at once. I imagined cinemagoers struggling to see the top of the actors' heads over the subtitles. I was slowly realising how strange it must be to live in a country with so many official languages. When the Swiss sat down of an evening to watch the news, they were watching three different programmes on three different channels. Swiss posties wear jackets with the name of their employer written on the back – three times: *Die Post*, *La Poste*, *La Posta*.

In the end I didn't see a film, but I did find myself in a restaurant called Movie, where the menu came on an empty film can and every dish was named after a flick. I ordered Chinatown (spring rolls) and The Godfather (pasta and chicken), but almost went for Breathless (garlic bread) and The Deep (prawn salad). Watching people having their own cinematic starters while joking with their friends, I felt a pang of homesickness for the first time. I'd been five weeks away, and I still had far to go. I envied these comfortable diners their rooted lives.

I passed the station on the way back to the guesthouse. People were sitting in a late local train, waiting for it to leave. Safe in their rectangles of light, they were going home to their husbands and wives, their comfy old sofas and their toothbrushes in the cup beside the bathroom wash-basin. I started to think about what I was going to do when I flew home from Milan in three weeks' time. Would this have been time off before I was forced to return to more conventional work, or the start of a new episode in my life? A crucial part of a pilgrimage seemed to be what happened when you came home – if you'd gone for a reason you should return changed in some way. What that change was supposed to be I had no idea, but I had three weeks to work it out.

With the sun shining on the mountain scenery it was downhill all the way to Arbon on the shores of Lake Constance. The road unwound gently, so I relaxed on the bike and let it take me there, marvelling over how beautiful it all was.

The trip computer had started to cut out – one minute the speed was forty k.p.h., the next it had dropped to zero. Since I'd left Dublin, it had been pestering me about how slowly I was going, but it had also loyally counted every last metre of the trip and had been a great help in parcelling out the day. I was sorry to see it failing, and made a couple of attempts to bring it back to life, but I was out of luck. From here on, I'd have to use the distances given on the Michelin maps.

Arbon is an ordinary town in an extraordinary location. The centre is a kilometre from the lake and it looks like the Swiss version of many an Irish town, strung out along the main road, with a clatter of shops and cars showing I'd arrived. People were bustling around with dogs and shopping-bags – but shouldn't they have been down on the shore looking at the water? When I stopped freewheeling I'd arrived beside the lake, and could see across the water to the high mountains in the east. The light was clear and sharp, with silver stars dancing on the lake's surface. I couldn't believe there weren't crowds of people there to see such a wonderful sight. I grew up about as far from the sea as you can get in England, so I've always been impatient with people who live beside large expanses of water and take them for granted.

After Arbon, navigation got a little complicated as three countries and a huge lake converged. Bregenz, sitting at the end of Lake Constance, is in Austria, but continue a little further round the lake and you're in Germany. Add in the signposts for Liechtenstein to the south, and things become even more confusing. I was crossing from Switzerland back into Euroland. I'd never really thought of the Austrians as my EU brothers, but the blue flag was flying over the customs post as the border guard asked to see my passport. The Irish harp had been worn away from the cover of my burgundy EU passport, so I tried to tell him where I was from.

'*Ich bin aus Irland,*' I smiled, making the country sound like 'eye-land'.

He looked troubled, but his visage cleared as he turned to the last page of the passport.

'Eerland, not Eye-land,' he said, and with my pronunciation corrected, I was waved on my way. I rode along cycle paths, through woods and out on to a bridge that spanned the Rhine as it joined the lake, having carved a wide valley down from the Alps.

My Bregenz guesthouse room was from the 1950s – heavy wooden furniture, peeling patterned wallpaper, metal-framed windows and linoleum on the floor. The shower down the hall was a grey tiled box, its only features the taps, shower-head and plug-hole. A naked lightbulb hung from the ceiling – it was the place for a violent interrogation. But the rest of the town was culturally rich, and blessed with a fine location between the wooded hills and the expanse of the lake. It offered an auditorium with a floating stage, lots of imaginative modern architecture and an old town back up the hill from the water. I sat on a bench overlooking the lake and had lunch watching the steamers come in and out. I was reminded of Bangor – a north-facing port with hills behind it.

Having made it over the mountains from Tuggen, Columbanus and his followers met a priest named Willimar in Arbon. After their time among the pagans, the monks must have been overjoyed to see him, and he was equally delighted to meet the pious foreigners who had walked out of the mountains to him. He welcomed them warmly, and they rested in Arbon for some time. Columbanus asked Willimar if there was a place nearby where they could found a monastery, as they'd promised Theudebert they would. Willimar described a place 'where are yet to be seen ruins of ancient buildings; the soil is rich and well-suited for crops, there are lofty mountains around, and adjoining the town is a wide and level expanse of waste land which will not deny to such as seek a living the fruits of their toil'. This was Bregenz, where the monks were to stay for two years, from 610 to 612.

The locals in the town followed a version of Christianity that was tinged with worship of the local gods, and the oratory to St Aurelia that the monks found contained bronze pagan images. Gall, who was yet to be blackballed, began to preach the Gospels a little more tactfully than he had in Tuggen. He broke the images with stones to show that no harm would come to people who chose to follow the Christian God. Some people were angry, but more were prepared to listen to the monks, who had soon built huts, a garden and an enclosure for cattle.

Today the church of St Gallus is up the hill behind the old town, on the site where the monastery was founded. Nestling in the trees, it has an elegant stone clock-tower topped with scrollwork, and while there's little sign of Gall except his name, two streets in the town are also named for the visiting Irishmen: Gallustrasse and Kolumbanstrasse curve down towards the lake, and the houses each have numbers on them that also give the street name. People still live in places that literally bear the mark of Columbanus and his friend.

Outside the Café Wunderbar, down near the lake, I was nearly undone by the complexity of foreign-exchange transactions. The menu listed prices in Austrian schillings and euros (which didn't exist yet), while my head was working in Irish pounds and Swiss francs; I had to translate the Swiss francs through French francs to arrive at a number

I understood. I handed over my schillings, and the waitress fumbled for my change. Not having enough schillings, she gave me the rest in Deutschmarks, which confused matters even further. Thank God for the euro.

20

Into the High Alps

The monks were soon well established in Bregenz, and they could scarcely have found a more picturesque spot. But once again Columbanus's enemies Theuderic and Brunhilda intervened. Theuderic went to war against his brother Theudebert, the monks' protector, and comprehensively defeated him. Things didn't look good for Columbanus, and the situation worsened when the local count, Gunzo, heard that the monks had now lost their royal sponsor and heeded local complaints about them. Some of the brothers had been walking far away from their lakeside enclosure, affecting the hunting, and there were also complaints that they were interfering with local customs. Things came to a head when one of the monastery's cows was deliberately released, and two monks went to bring it back. They were killed, and it was clear that Bregenz was no longer safe for Columbanus. After two years beside the lake, they gathered their things and set off again, this time for Italy.

For me, Milan was a week's ride away. Suddenly the trip seemed nearly done, but the most difficult cycling challenge was still ahead. I couldn't avoid the big mountains any longer. As I rode out of Bregenz, all I could see to the south were peaks, piling up in ridges with each set higher than the last. The climbs up to St Gallen from Lake Zurich had been hard but short; from here, I'd be going uphill for three days.

I had no idea what it was going to be like up there. Since the planning days in Dublin, I'd known I would have to cross the Alps, but (perhaps wisely) I had not thought about what that would mean, preferring to deal with it later. Now it was later, and although I'd survived the early climbs on the way to St Gallen, what lay ahead was sure to be much harder. I wasn't dawdling along the Loire in the summer sun any more.

And, to use a technical term, I was riding like a bag of spanners. Out of Bregenz on busy roads, I quickly grew to hate Austrian truck drivers – two had pulled out in front of me within five minutes. As the road passed through the fringes of grey towns, the cycle path crossed the entrances to supermarket car parks and car dealerships. I was sure I was going to be T-boned by a family estate as the driver pulled out while putting on his seatbelt and talking on his mobile. With the trip computer not working, at least I couldn't tell how slowly I was riding. My legs were heavy and my head slightly fuzzy, which I put down to the beer and MSG cocktail of the previous night's meal. Chinese food is famously good value in Austria, so after a week's overpriced Swiss fare I had joined Bregenz's Oriental community to over-indulge at a small restaurant near my guesthouse.

So it was a grumpy cyclist who sought the civility and quiet of Switzerland, dodging back across the Rhine at the first opportunity. The peaks on either side of the broad valley floor grew higher and higher, and the sun briefly appeared from between the grey clouds. I'd been riding in my longs and waterproof for so long now that I yearned for some good weather to warm my bones – Italy couldn't come soon enough.

But first I came to the principality of Liechtenstein. Only twenty-five kilometres long and around six across, it's even more wealthy than its Swiss neighbour, offering employment to the relatively impoverished guest workers, who cross the border every day in their big Audis. The capital, Vaduz, is a strange amalgam of strip mall and *The Sound of Music* strung out along the main road south. The postcard scenery and moody royal fortress atop a rocky crag jar with the low-slung modern office buildings below it, which house the banks and offshore traders largely responsible for the principality's wealth. Liechtenstein has a population of thirty thousand, but eighty thousand registered companies. Tourism is also a money-spinner. There are no border regulations if you enter from Switzerland, but if you want a Liechtenstein stamp in your passport, you have to pay for it at the tourist office.

The business-oriented approach to running the country has resulted in a unique opportunity for the person who has everything. Looking for an extra-special venue for your next party or corporate event? Why not rent a whole country? The deal stops short of turfing out all the locals and giving you the run of the place, but apparently for a little under 250,000 euros a night it's now possible to rent Liechtenstein. You can fly your own flag in place of the official one, and up to nine hundred of your closest friends can stay with host families throughout the principality. And if you don't believe me, you can go to the Rent-a-State website for all the information.

I had lunch sitting on a bench in the centre of town,

watching coachloads of American and German tourists waddling to and from the main street. The scenery around Vaduz was worth coming to see, but being in the middle of town was the best way to avoid it. As I wheeled the bike towards the main road again, I was stopped on the pavement at a junction when a slight, bookish man approached me and asked me a question in German. I fumbled for a reply, and he tried again in English. 'You are on holiday, yes?'

'That's right.'

He then asked me the question I was becoming increasingly proud to answer: 'How far do you go?' I told him, and his face shone. 'That's excellent. Great. And which way do you go over the mountains?'

'Over the Splugen Pass,' I told him.

'Yes! Amazing, that route. Down to Comosee, the Lake of Como.'

'That's right.' My mood was lifting rapidly.

'Well, enjoy your trip. It is great.'

He waved and smiled, then crossed the street. Where had he come from? It was as if he'd been told to stand there and wait for a cyclist on a touring bike to come past so he could cheer me up. I might not feel at my best, and the day so far had been a dull grind, but I was in Liechtenstein of all places, and strangers were stopping me to tell me that what I was doing was great.

A little way from town the landscape reasserted itself, and the mountains reappeared. The campsite was up a quiet side road at the base of a steep ridge. The office was closed, but a sign told campers to pick a spot on the terraced site and come back to register later. Up went my tent and I snoozed while I waited to sign in. I woke up hungry. I didn't fancy a trip back into Vaduz to eat, so my only hope was a restaurant I'd spotted just down from the campsite, but I feared it might be closed on a Thursday night in late September. Might as well give it a lash. After signing in, I wandered down the dark lane, clutching my book as if I knew where I was going. There was a stream running alongside the road, its waters chattering as it tumbled downhill. A few large houses were hidden up long gravel driveways, their living-room windows facing west to the peaks across the valley.

I was in luck. Diners were sitting in the large windows of the wooden building. Outside it looked like a giant log cabin, but inside it was bright and airy. Underdressed again – they hid me at a table near the bar, away from the smartest clients round the corner in the dining room.

As I strolled back up the hill, the air was sharper and the stars were out. From beneath a hedge I heard a rustling, and a tortoiseshell cat appeared. I bent down and held out my hand to him. He came over to investigate. He looked like George, the cat I'd loved and lost. Before I'd left for America, I'd taken in a kitten, and brought him up the best way I could. I was a single-parent family, but I tried to make time for him, and he grew up to be a sweet young cat, purring and approachable. But then I noticed he was spending less time at home, and some nights he didn't come home at all. When he was back, we pretended everything was fine, but then he'd be off again, and I knew not to ask where he was going.

Things weren't great between us, but then I didn't see him at all for three days. Late in the afternoon, I was in the kitchen and he came over the back fence. I was shocked by what I saw. He was wearing a new red velvet collar. George had left me. This was just a courtesy visit, to see how I was getting along. He came in, and I examined a shiny tag hanging from the blood-red collar. A Dublin phone number was printed on it, and a second number with the Kerry area code. I'd done my best for that cat, and he'd chosen to be with someone who could offer him something I never could – a weekend place in the country.

As the Alpine cat approached, I could see that he didn't really look like George. He sniffed my hand briefly, then sauntered back into the hedge. 'Go on,' I said. 'Just walk away. Like you all do, eventually.'

Each night it was getting dark earlier, and I was soon sitting in the tent with my torch on my head, scribbling in my notebook. It was eight thirty. By eleven it was raining hard, but I was warm in my sleeping-bag, listening to the World Service. The radio had been an excellent companion, making everywhere feel a bit like home.

It was still raining when I woke up, and I had to do some damp juggling to get the tent down. But even with the extra weight of sodden nylon in my panniers I was in good spirits as I rolled out of the campsite. The rain stopped a little way up the road, and three fighter jets powered above me, close to the valley floor. I was still just in Liechtenstein, but the planes were on the Swiss side of the river. I'd never thought of the Swiss having an air force, but I knew of their hard-ass attitude to self-defence. Every Swiss man has a rifle in his wardrobe: once he's completed the mandatory national service he gets to keep the gun, and regular shooting tests ensure that he remembers how to use it. In other countries, a heavily armed populace has proved a bad idea, but it works here.

This constitutes one strand of the Swiss 'Don't mess with

us' attitude, the other being, 'We've got all your money'. They've only recently voted to join the United Nations, and this commitment to neutrality seemed to trickle down to everyday dealings with outsiders like myself. Everyone was helpful and polite, but few were friendly. They just wanted to be left alone, and would treat you as if you wanted the same thing, even if you didn't.

Bregenz was now over seventy kilometres behind me, and while the peaks on either side were getting steadily higher, the valley floor was only rising slightly. It was great cycling sleight-of-hand to be so far into the mountains without having to go up any of them, but as I spun along the rapidly drying roads I knew I was overdue some serious uppage. The first payback came on the way into Chur (Huuuggghrr), when the road steepened markedly. The heavy bags pulled back on the bike, and I was working harder to ride more slowly. It wasn't so steep that I would have to get off and push, but I wasn't sure how long I could stay at this level of effort over the higher mountains. Fortunately, Chur arrived before I had to find out.

The town marks the start of the high Alps, and serves as the main junction for the transport links in the area. From here the roads divide as they struggle up into the thin air – straight on for St Moritz, right then left for the Splugen and San Bernadino passes, keep right for the Oberalp and the St Gotthard passes. Chur itself was much more pleasant than it sounded, with a busy pedestrianised main drag, and some elegant nineteenth-century buildings. I stole a look at a newspaper over lunch – the weather forecast was for rain and cloud over the next few days. This might be a problem, as I didn't fancy climbing up to 2100 metres in freezing rain, or picking my way down wet hairpin bends on the Italian side of the border.

But that afternoon it was warm and sunny, and as I watched office workers laughing over their lunches, I felt no sense of being in the mountains. These people had slept in their warm beds last night and caught the tram to work; the weather was only of passing interest to them. At this time of year, their lives were untouched by being in the Alps. Meanwhile I was checking the pressure and altitude on my watch, and wondering if my legs and lungs could cope with what lay ahead.

On the way up to Thusis, the gradient was permanent but gradual enough that I could find a rhythm and stick to it. As the town approached, the valley narrowed and the road rose more steeply. So far so good on the climbing, but I was still only at 700 metres.

Thusis was little more than a main street, but the hotels spoke of a good ski trade in the winter. Mine had the slightly run-down feel of a small-town establishment that doesn't have to fight for business, but the landlady let me park the bike in the family garage and I was soon upstairs looking out of my window. Over the rough roof of the house next door I could see a dense pine forest that stretched up a steep slope. Behind that was the huge snow-capped summit of the nearest alp. It looked like the imperious peak at the start of Paramount Pictures films. That was a mountain. And that was where I was going.

I added some Alpine-specific disasters to my original list of all the bad things that would happen to me: my brake lever might fall off in my hands on a steep descent and I'd go straight over the barrier as the road turned; innocent Swiss children on their way home from school would watch in horror as I tumbled down the snowy mountain. Or my legs might seize up in a giant cramp brought on by the relentless climbing, leaving me miles from the top in the dark with a storm rolling in. Out here on my own, no one would even know to look for me. Why had I thought I could do this?

It was time to distract myself with some Columbanus reading. Unfortunately Jonas says almost nothing about the monks' journey over the Alps. 'When Columbanus saw that Theudebert had been conquered by Theuderic, he left Gaul and Germany and went to Italy,' is all we get about the arduous journey through beautiful but dangerous terrain. But Jonas's purpose was not to provide a complete bio-graphy of the saint's life, but to offer proof of his sanctity, and an encouragement to others. Miracles win out over facts. There's no word of the route he took after Chur, but the Splugen Pass is the conclusion of most of the experts.

By this point Columbanus was in his sixties, and the name of the road just outside Thusis gives some sense of the rigour of the journey. The valley narrowed to a ravine, and the road was cut into the side of the mountain, ending up more like a rough flight of steps than a major thoroughfare. A fast-flowing river filled the bottom of the ravine, and the weather was frequently wild. There were precious few settlements from here until you were heading down on the other side. This stretch of the route is still known as the 'Via Mala' – the bad road.

I called ahead to Splugen – the settlement closest to the top of the pass – and made a reservation for the following night. However, the television in my room had confirmed the weather forecast in the Chur newspaper. It was to be dry the next day, but rainy and cold after that. I hatched a plan. So far my daily cycling goals had been modest, hardly more than a hundred kilometres a day on flattish roads. The bigger achievement lay in just turning up at the bike every day and riding; I'd climbed hills when I'd had to, but I'd never (to use a cycling idiom) really put the hammer down. I'd keep the reservation in Splugen, but the plan was to complete the twenty-six kilometres up to Splugen early ('up' being the operative word, of course), then keep going to the top of the pass and down the other side to Chiavenna. I'd overcome the Via Mala, arrive in Italy in style, and avoid the nasty weather. If I could do it.

It was time to borrow some of Columbanus's rigour and indestructible self-belief. He had been a pensioner when he arrived here, and had been driven out of two monasteries in the previous three years. He and his followers were on foot, and he would never have seen such high peaks as these. I could imagine him setting a ferocious pace, leaving younger men behind, his Roy Keane face on.

I woke early, excited and anxious. I wolfed down as much muesli, bread and cheese as I could manage – as Roy Keane says, 'Fail to prepare, prepare to fail.' Outside, the Saturday-morning bustle was beginning in the high street, and I pushed the bike along the pavement towards the super-market. Each action seemed more significant than normal. The supermarket was busy, but I dodged the trolleys and found the energy bars and sports drinks. How much fuel do you need to ride up steep hills for hours? I bought a box of eight bars and enough liquid to fill both my bottles with some left over.

Back outside I was getting ready to leave when a couple approached me. They asked where I was going, and I told them. The woman blew out her cheeks. 'But it is like this,' she said, tilting her arm at a steep angle.

'I know,' was the best reply I could manage.

She looked at her husband, and then back at me. Clearly she thought I was mad. Hatstand, fish, banana. Her face clouded as she tried to work out why I would want to do this. 'Like this,' she repeated, her fingers pointed skyward.

'I've ridden across France to get here. I have to go up there,' I said thinly.

She shook her head, and said, 'Good luck.' She still didn't get it. I wasn't sure I did either. But I'd volunteered myself for this, and there was no getting out of it now. Like one of Columbanus's monks, or Roy Keane's international team-mates, I had to follow the example of the stern leader and try to perform above myself.

Out of town, the road ran down a slight hill, then entered the ravine. Modern highway engineering had done away with the steps, replacing them with winding narrow tunnels. It was horrible to ride a bike through them with coaches and cars swerving out to avoid me. My legs weren't warmed up, and the tunnels had a sharp incline, and I emerged each time more annoyed than the last. I rounded a corner with a truck right behind me, and saw cars parked all over the road ahead, and a coach manoeuvring into a lay-by. It was the Via Mala visitor centre – you could walk down and explore a section of the original track.

I was already on my own bad road, and it was too early in

the day to stop, so I kept on slogging, with my heart-rate much faster than I wanted at this stage. But soon the valley and road widened, and I could relax a little as I turned off onto the old road, which started climbing in earnest. Most of the traffic stayed on the main road, which became a dual carriageway, speeding drivers up towards the San Bernadino Pass as if it were the South Mimms service station on the M25 around London.

Everyone has their own way of riding up hills. Some attack them from the bottom in a big gear, honking away out of the saddle as if to get as far as they can up the slope before their legs and lungs have realised they're going uphill – like Wile E. Coyote trying to run in mid-air: it's fine so long as you don't look down. Others start slowly, then wind it up as they get closer to the top, their aim being to arrive at the summit in time to breathe their last mortal breath. If you're racing, you can try a few more approaches. The great Miguel Indurain, who should have been much too big to be any good in the mountains, had a habit of dropping his fellow riders gradually. Without seeming to modify his steady pedal stroke, he'd slowly edge away from the group, grinding their morale as they struggled to match him. Lance Armstrong pushes a lighter gear more quickly, and has an astonishing ability to come out of the saddle and dance away from his opponents. These explosive attacks snap the elastic that keeps groups together, and Armstrong can gain enough time in a couple of kilometres to keep him clear for the rest of the stage.

My aim, however, was different: survival. On the heavy-assed tourer, I found an easy gear (the second easiest I had – I wanted the granny gear in case I needed it later) and started spinning, trying not to push too hard early on. I had no idea how deep into my reserves I'd have to go before the day was out, so I didn't worry about how quickly I was travelling – I just kept admiring the scenery as the road rose into a wider set of meadows. Through the village of Andeer, the map showed the yellow line zigzagging madly for the next kilometre, the hairpins piling on top of each other like folds of ribbon. After I'd rounded the first two, I could look back over my shoulder at the drop beneath me – it was steep but I could manage it. A car approached from behind and downshifted as we both came into the next switchback. I got out of the saddle and increased the pace a little to show the lardy car-drivers that this was no bother to me, but as soon as they were gone, I slowed down again, my heart pounding. Vanity's a terrible thing.

As the road straightened, it entered another broad valley – the mountains rose in steps, with each valley higher than the last. For Columbanus each climb must have seemed like the final one until he reached the top of the slope to see still more frightening peaks rising in the distance. I was now around 1400 metres up, but all around were snow-covered mountains that reached as far again into the sky. The dual carriageway reappeared, heading straight for Splugen, which I could see in the distance. The minor road had a few more kinks in it, but I arrived in the village and found my way to a restaurant for soup and pasta. I was in reasonable shape, but daunted by what lay ahead.

But you already know what that is – so skip back to the first chapter to read it again, or come with me quickly as I guts it up the final ten kilometres into the snow and mist at the top of the Splugen Pass, and speed down the other side into black tunnels and vicious hairpins to arrive shaking and stirred into terracotta Chiavenna near the north end of Lake Como. Ireland to Italy on a bike – how do you like them apples?

21

Bella Italia

I was still buzzing as I called my sister from the hotel room. Words tumbling over each other, I ran through the day's achievement, tired but still excited like a child leaving a funfair. I kept talking and talking, wanting to share this moment, to express my gratitude for being there.

Uma told me she was proud of me, which was the first time anyone had ever said that to me. And, just as novel, I realised I was proud of myself. Whatever happened from here, I'd always be the person who had ridden a bike from Bangor, across France and Switzerland and over snowy peaks to Italy. It might not mean much to others, but I'd set out to do something difficult, and now I had done it. So *this* was what a feeling of accomplishment was like. I couldn't stop grinning. One of my water-bottles had collapsed in on itself from the pressure difference between the top of the pass and the bottom.

Chiavenna was overcast and misty as I walked around deciding where to have my celebration meal. The town was surrounded on three sides by tree-covered slopes, and I caught glimpses of them as I turned corners in the narrow cobbled streets. Everyone was in their finery for the Saturday-evening *passeggiata*. Small squares opened at intervals, and I was soon happily lost. I ended up at a trattoria with white walls, a vaulted ceiling and windows that looked out on the narrow river that ran through the town. The water had started up at the top of the mountains, where I'd just come from. The morning's grim hotel in Thusis was another country.

Ah, Italian food, Italian restaurants. For tonight at least, all was right in my world, and the veggie *antipasti* and great polenta and grilled fish simply confirmed this. It was a Saturday night in a place I'd never been before, and I felt right at home. Columbanus's last resting-place was just a week away.

My next resting-place, however, would not have pleased the saint. I was lying in the bath of my room in Bellagio watching the Tour of Spain on the television through the open bathroom door. There was no monastic asceticism in the Hotel Metropole, so I'd plumped for a room with a balcony that looked straight out over Lake Como. The sounds of the steamers' deep horns and chugging engines floated up through the open doors. I'd pushed the boat out so I could watch the boats come in as I lay on my bed.

Rain had been misting down all day. It was much warmer here than up in the mountains, but clouds still sat on top of the hills, with wisps of cotton-wool nestling in the wooded hollows. If it was like this down here, it would have been miserable up at Splugen – I'd made the right choice in pressing on. On a crappy day Lake Como still looked beautiful.

On the way from Chiavenna to the steamer landing at Colico, a group of road cyclists had passed me in a soggy swish of coloured Lycra. My legs were tender from the previous day's effort, but the four roadies weren't going that much faster than me, so I upped my speed a little and the gap between us stabilised for a while. Slowly, they edged away again and I magnanimously let them go. A little later, the road carved a broad curve and there were the guys, stopped beside a German-registered camper van, their hands cupped round mugs of coffee. They smiled and waved as I passed.

Colico was the most northerly stop the ferries made, and I was worried I wouldn't be able to take the bike on board. The timetable at the jetty said there was a fast boat in a couple of hours, with a slower steamer half an hour later. There was no one in the ticket office to ask about the bike, so some lunch was in order.

My wet cycling stuff was a little conspicuous in the lakeside restaurant. I was wearing my grungy mountain-biking gear that made me look as if I was attending a muddy music festival. But I was not as obvious as my German friends, who arrived a little later in their clinging bright Lycra. They came over for a quick chat. They were crossing chunks of Italy in the camper van, then getting out and riding in the picturesque spots. Lake Garda was next, and eventually they'd end up in Rome. It was a good way to travel, because riding a tourer doesn't give you a great deal of cycling pleasure if you're used to the taut and frisky fun of a good racing bike.

After lunch there was no problem getting on the nearly empty ferry, and the rain cleared for a time as we chugged down the narrow lake. The steep, wooded hillsides slid down to the water, with small villages on the shore here and there. As we got further south the size of the settlements increased and more people got on, until in the distance the lake forked and a town emerged from the mist at the apex of the spit of land. Bellagio, beloved of the English Romantics, praised in poetry and song. Villas and coral-coloured hotels lined the shore, and when we landed I brazenly clip-clopped into one of the grander establishments and enquired if they had a room, and where could I leave my bike?

In Ireland, people assume you're riding a bike because you have no money – certainly not enough to stay in swanky Italian hotels – which needn't be true. Dave, my cycling friend, drives an old Renault Clio, and when he puts his Specialized S-Works racing bike in the back (with its Mavic Ksyrium wheels and Dura-Ace components), he has more than doubled the value of the car. You can easily pay a thousand euros for a set of wheels if you're so inclined, and not much of the other kit comes cheap either: helmets, shoes, pedals, gloves, sunglasses, shorts, jerseys, socks. Magazines offer pages of bike porn – reviews of the latest carbon-fibre seatposts, and frames made of the same ceramic particulate they use in the engines of tanks. The law of diminishing returns applies, but by and large a fifteen-hundred-euro bike will perform considerably better than a cheaper one, proving more reliable, faster, lighter and easier to maintain.

However, there's an unwritten law that says you're expec-ted to perform as well as your kit. A weekend warrior is breaking the rules if he blows five thousand euros on a handsome titanium Merlin bike and only rides it to the shops to get the paper. There are few enough people like this in Ireland, but during a visit to Los Angeles I witnessed the most impressive display of bike hardware I'd seen since the Tour de France started in Dublin in 1998.

It was a Saturday morning and the bikes were leaning up against the wall outside a branch of Noah's Bagels in the upscale neighbourhood of Brentwood, between Beverly Hills and Santa Monica. There were stylish Italian steeds from Bianchi and Colnago, Lance Armstrong-approved full-carbon techno-triumphs from Trek, and various other high-end Giants, Lemonds, Litespeeds and Cannondales. Their owners were sitting at the outside tables soaking up the sun in their pro kit.

I asked my companion where the group rode to, this being one of the most sprawling and car-friendly cities in the world.

'Mostly just down to the beach.'

'How far is that?'

'About three miles. But they come back up as well.'

I looked more closely at the bike-owners, with their Rudy Project shades balanced on top of their heads. Many were carrying a bit of excess baggage round their waists and in their upper arms. Some excellent cyclists are big – tree-trunk legs and barrel-chests – but there's no extra fat on them. This crowd looked soft.

'But there must be longer rides they go on – you wouldn't break a sweat in three miles,' I said.

'Not really. They're more or less penned in around here by freeways and the ocean.'

Relaxing at a café after a good ride is one of the joys of cycling. Dublin is particularly amenable to this: you can be dying a thousand deaths on the sharp climbs up in the Wicklow mountains at eleven o'clock, and enjoying coffee and a slice of pear tart outside Bar Italia by eleven thirty. But the LA guys just cut out the suffering – why not ride your five-grand bike straight to the bagel place?

But I digress. I was standing in the reception of the smart hotel in my thrasher-dude cycling duds. It was a rainy Sunday afternoon at the end of the season, so the demure receptionist gracefully ignored my unconventional attire, and checked me in, explaining that I could lock the bike on the covered terrace outside. A humble English tourer can seldom have had such an impressive billet. It spent the night leaning up against an ornate railing, staring out across the lake; I imagined it dressed in a dinner suit with a martini resting nonchalantly on the handlebars.

I tried not to hit the well-heeled tourists with my muddy panniers on the way up the stairs, and was soon standing on the balcony looking back up the lake. Actually, with all the mist, there wasn't much of a view but that scarcely mattered. The bathroom had the first bath I'd seen since Zurich, and the television was showing a mountain stage from the Tour of Spain. A joyful combination for a tired cyclist. Much better to soak in the hot water and let the pros do the work.

Back from the lake shore, the town rose steeply up the hill, with narrow flights of steps connecting the wider streets that wound their way across the slope. But straying too far from my fantastic room seemed a waste, so after dinner I hurried back to lie on the bed with the balcony doors open and watch the last of the boats arrive for the night, the water lapping around their hulls like gentle applause. Across the dark water I could see the shimmering lights of nearby towns. When I woke in the middle of the night, I barefooted out to the balcony and sat there for a while, until I got too cold and retreated back under the covers.

Next morning I waited around for as long as I could, getting every last minute's use of my lovely view. I had dashed down to the dining room to load up at the breakfast buffet. Most of the other guests were older English and American couples, and a chipper young waiter was schmoozing them as he delivered the coffee. Then I sat on my balcony writing postcards and fending off the cleaners. Last checkout was at eleven, and at ten fifty-five I presented my key and credit card at the desk. It was undoubtedly the best hotel stay of the trip.

The road to the city of Como winds alongside the lake all the way, passing through small villages nestled against the steep hills. For the first time in weeks I rode without my waterproof on, and there was a softness and warmth to the air that was beguiling after the sharper bite of the Alpine weather. The route I was taking is still known as the Via Regina – the Queen's Road – named for Theodelinda, the Catholic wife of the Lombard king Agilulf who was ruling when the Irishmen arrived over the mountains. As with the Franks in France, the Lombards were a barbarian tribe who had seized the opportunity to invade when the Roman Empire fractured in the fifth century. Their conquest of much of northern Italy was speedy and brutal, but life in most of the cities continued largely untouched, and Agilulf proved himself an able ruler. He ascribed to the Aryan heresy, but his wife Theodelinda was a Catholic, and it seems that it was she who welcomed the monks to the court in Milan.

You might think that Columbanus would have had enough of mixing with royalty after his experiences with Theuderic – he'd already been forced to leave two homes as the power of his sponsors waxed and waned. But for a man so convinced of the inherent sinfulness of the temporal world, he seems to have been drawn again and again to its powerful leaders. Their morals and values were different from his own, and life at court was different from the remote caves in which he seems to have been equally at home. However, for an Irishman, monasteries were royal foundations, and all Columbanus's time in France never taught him to respect the diocesan hierarchy of the Church. If you wanted land for a monastery in Ireland, you'd go to the local king, which was exactly what Columbanus did on his arrival in Italy.

He might not have had much time for bishops, but he still thought of himself as a loyal and devout Catholic. He spent part of his time in Milan weighing in on the Pope's side in doctrinal disputes. The letters he wrote at the time show his passion in the matter, even if his grasp of the intricacies of the debate was less than perfect. Columbanus was loyal to the Pope, but in a way that suggested God's representative on earth could still stand to learn a few things. As early as 600, Columbanus had taken issue with one of the most accomplished popes of the era, Gregory the Great, respectfully telling him that he was wrong over the calculation of Easter. In 613, in a letter written after his arrival in Italy, Columbanus put Pope Boniface IV straight on a few details. He started simply enough: 'For all we Irish, inhabitants of the world's edge, are disciples of Ss Peter and Paul,' but he had found that in Italy, 'the rulers of this province have long trampled on the Catholic faith and consolidated this lapse into Aryanism'. Columbanus was clear that the current incumbent of the Holy See was failing in his duty: 'Watch, dear Pope, it is time to arise from sleep.'

Of course, at the same time as he was complaining to the

Pope for not doing enough about the Aryan heresy, he was staying at the court of the chief trampler on the faith. Personally, Agilulf seems to have been flexible and tolerant towards those of his wife's faith, and Columbanus had a wide practical streak in him. His commitment to his monks was such that he would do anything to secure a future for them. Taking gifts from a heretical king presented no problems to him.

If Columbanus was received royally when he reached the south end of the lake, I had a more troubled arrival. The city of Como draws a lot of tourists on their way to many parts of the lake, but doesn't seem to have many hotels. 'If you can find a room, take it immediately, whatever it costs,' advised one hotelier, as he turned me away. I ended up in a thread-bare double room in a hotel back from the water. The man at the reception desk scarcely looked up from his paper as he handed me the key and told me there was nowhere to put the bike. My companion had to make do with being locked to a railing on the street outside.

Como was home to Alessandro Volta, and electricians will be delighted to hear that his statue is well illuminated. It needed to be: the rainy gloom had returned, enveloping the small square named for the scientist. I seemed to have a cartoon black cloud following me around, and I retreated to a bar there. My Peroni came with a bowl of crisps and some slices of bread with tomato and basil, and I scribbled a few lines in my notebook while I waited for the worst of the rain to pass. It was ten years since I'd been in an Italian town of this size, and it felt good to be back among the attractive mix of architecture and anarchy. I decided to take a day off in Como and explore.

★

Next morning things weren't going well in the post office. All I wanted was to post my bundle of Swiss maps and books and pick up some stamps for postcards. I handed over my package to the woman behind the counter and said, '*Per Irlanda, per favore.*' She looked blank. I'm in a post office with a big envelope with an address on it. I'm unlikely to be looking for a haircut. I tried again, '*Questo per Irlanda? Ireland? Ah, come on ...*'

She shrugged her shoulders and told me she didn't understand. Whatever the woman was being paid, it clearly wasn't enough that she could buy herself a clue. Asking for stamps for postcards (in what I thought was passable Italian) was the last straw, and I was handed on to someone else. The new woman was much more helpful and I left the post office with my stamps, but also with the suspicion that I'd never see my guidebook to Switzerland again. My Latin teacher at school had told a similar story of breakdown in communication. When he was in Rome, he'd found himself in a baker's, looking for a loaf of bread. Surrounded by the produce of the baker's oven, my teacher had reached the front of the queue and said, '*Buon giorno. Pane, per favore.*' The baker's assistant just looked at him.

'*Pane,*' he tried again. Still nothing.

He pointed to a loaf. '*Pane?*'

The assistant's face broadened into a smile of understanding. '*Ah! Si! Pane!*'

My next stop was the Black Dragon Internet café, although the name makes it sound more respectable than it was. A handwritten sign in the window of an unprepossessing café-bar-tobacconist led me in and down the stairs.

David Moore

The basement was part store-room, part bar and part global-telecommunications hub. Tables and chairs were stacked next to cardboard boxes. Fading beer posters covered the walls, featuring 1980s models in frayed denim shorts and shirts knotted across their midriffs. In the corner a table contained three no-name PCs. A young English couple were sitting at one, and next to them was a large black-clad woman with long brown hair. A bookish man with a clipboard was standing over them. He told me to sit down at the spare machine, then disappeared upstairs.

I filed my story about climbing the Alps and checked my mail while the English couple were arguing politely about the email they were writing. 'I don't know about that. "Having a lovely time" sounds so fake,' said the girl.

'What?'

'It sounds like we don't really mean it. That's what you put when you can't think of anything to say,' she said.

The guy looked confused. 'But we are having a lovely time, aren't we?'

'Yes, we are, but I think we should say "fantastic", in case they think we're covering something up.'

'What could we be covering up? We only got married three days ago.'

'Well, you know what some people are like. They read too much into things,' she said.

'You don't say. OK, there, I've put in "fantastic" for you.'

'And don't forget the exclamation marks. That'll show what a lovely time we're having.'

The woman next to me was pounding away on the keyboard with hands of concrete and fingernails of deep purple. She paused and started similarly hostile mousing

236

before letting out a thunderous 'Shit! I don't believe it. I've lost my whole frigging mail!'

'Um,' I ventured. This was one angry American. 'Are you using Hotmail?'

'Yep. I clicked Send and now it's hung. Where's that Italian guy? I was writing that mail for thirty minutes.'

The couple stopped bickering and started making sympathetic noises.

'Have you tried clicking the Back button on the browser? It should bring you back to the page you were on before,' I suggested.

'Could I lose everything, though?'

'Yeah, that's possible.'

I held my breath as she clicked on the Back button. A page of text appeared on the screen.

She beamed and softened. 'That's it! Thanks very much.'

'No problem.'

She turned back to the machine, and started pounding away again, adding to the bottom of the mail. As I was walking up the stairs, the newlyweds were at it again: 'If your friend Tony couldn't be bothered to make it to the wedding, I don't see why he should get an email from us now.'

The American woman slammed a hand on the desk. 'It's done it again!'

I scampered up the last two steps and through the door. They were the first native English speakers I'd come across for weeks. The thought of returning home didn't make me very happy.

By mid-afternoon I'd completed all my admin, and I adjourned to the Bar Touring near the lake. It had large windows looking out on to the piazza and a red marble bar with mirrored bays for glasses and bottles. It was still busy with tourists and well-dressed locals finishing their lunch, shopping-bags lying around their feet like loyal hounds. A man in a raincoat was standing at the bar knocking back an espresso, and one of the barmen nodded to me as I sat down at a small table. All the staff were in their forties or above, dressed in white shirts with patterned waistcoats and bow-ties. They moved with the same unflappable professionalism as the older barmen in good Dublin pubs.

One brought over my coffee. To me now it was as much ritual as beverage: I'd been powered by the stuff all the way from Dublin, and had grown to love the sound of the snorting espresso machine at work.

By the time I'd finished, the quality of the light had changed. The floor was now shining brightly and my car-toon cloud had finally departed. Outside, it was a different city. The water of the lake had turned from dirty grey to deep blue, with stars of light flashing as the breeze caught it. The trees on the hills were a deep rich green, offset by the azure of the sky, and the locals had all found their sunglasses. Back in the square near the hotel, Volta had dried off and was looking happier, although the Roman senator's robes he was wearing must have been a real pain to keep clean in the laboratory.

I had a leisurely afternoon nap, and woke to the sounds of the street through the open window: the whine of scooter engines, horns honking, elderly women greeting friends as they passed with their shopping, the steady ticking of an old bike ridden slowly. I lay there staring up at the high ceiling, happily trying to identify all the noises. Maybe I hadn't paid too much for the room.

22

Friends and Founders

As I had ridden through France and Switzerland, no one I met had any idea who I was. They took me as they found me – most often a perspiring Englishman with a cyclist's tan and a worried look. But riding out of Como on my way southeast, I was going to meet someone who knew me. Primrose lived in a small village near Monza, to the east of Milan, and though she'd been in Italy for perhaps thirty years, she'd been part of the diaspora that saw my mother and most of her friends leave Ireland in the 1960s. Primrose had met Bruno, a handsome young Italian, while they were both in London; she'd returned to Italy with him, and had been there ever since, making a home for themselves and their two daughters.

I'd first met them at the Sunday parties my parents held while I was growing up. A decade went by and the next time I saw Primrose was when I arrived in her village with my two friends while we were Interrailing around Europe between school and college. We'd just escaped from Basle youth hostel and had tried to sleep on the overnight train to Milan. In the small hours, I had woken to find a man with his hand in the front right pocket of my jeans. I think he was trying to extract my passport, but I was half asleep so anything's possible. When he saw I'd woken up, he calmly removed his hand, stepped back and slid the compartment door shut behind him.

My friends and I had spent the early hours of the morning sliding down the marble banisters of the stairs in Mussolini's lavish station in Milan, and had then caught a local train out to Primrose's. We stayed for a few days, and she dealt with the three of us with unending grace and practicality, sending us up to Bergamo and back into Milan during the day, and joining us for long meals around the big table in the evenings. I'd only seen her once since then, but when she arrived to meet me in the main piazza of the village, I recognised her immediately.

'*Ciao*, David. So you found us all right? It's good to see you. Just follow me back to the house.'

She drove home, and I tried to keep up on the bike, feeling slightly the worse for wear after the slog from Como. Cycling in Italy was closer to the Irish experience than the Swiss or French. The roads were potholed and narrow, and as I had approached the outskirts of Milan, the traffic volume increased markedly. I'd left the quiet lake-shore spins behind me, and was wrestling with big trucks and their unpredictable habits. Stopping in Monza hadn't been a good idea – it had taken me twenty minutes of confusion to find the centre of town, and when I got there the cathedral was closed for renovation. Inside it were some treasures from Queen Theodelinda's court, but unless I had a hard hat and a shovel, I wasn't getting in. As I arrived at Primrose's I realised I hadn't been in a house since I left Dublin. So this was how real people lived.

The next day I was in Milan, feeling vulnerable to the

crowds and the noise – I'd lost my protective covering somewhere along the hundreds of miles of country roads, and as I approached the Duomo, I was picked up and carried in the flow of tourists. I had a list of churches to see that had been around in Columbanus's time, but as I started out for the first, my heart wasn't really in it. I dutifully took the required photographs, but this close to Bobbio, I just wanted to be there, not traipsing round a city feeling sorry for myself. I could do that at home.

The next day, to be fair to them, the trucks meant well on the way south. When there was nothing coming the other way, they'd swing out and leave lots of room, and a lone cyclist only had to avoid being blown off the road by the massive draught they created. But when a large vehicle was thundering down the other side of the road (which was most of the time), there wasn't room for two wide loads and a touring bike. And the drivers weren't going to slow down, so I just had to concentrate on riding in a straight line an inch from the verge and hold her steady while the roaring roadship muscled past.

It's tempting to imagine Italy as a lightweight country beside the industrial solidity of Germany, for example. As if all that's made there is ice-cream, shoes and beautiful foot-ballers. But on the red road from Melzo to Melegnano, a lot of heavy objects were being shifted. You ride more quickly on a busy road, and I sped across the broad Lombard plain, making for Piacenza.

With a hazy sun and no wind, it was perfect weather for putting in the kilometres. After Melegnano the quieter roads gave me a chance to look around at the landscape. The harvest was in, and the brown fields were reduced to stubble, with shed-sized rolls of straw in the corners like giant bobbins. Clear of the trucks, the only danger came from the lazy squadrons of insects that clattered against my sunglasses as I rode into them. Nearly seventy kilometres had come and gone when I stopped at a sign announcing the name of a town just north of the Po river. I balanced the camera on a post on the side of the road and dashed over to stand in front of the sign: San Colombano al Lambro – the town had been named for Columbanus.

Local legend has it that the saint came through here on his way up to found the monastery at Bobbio, and that he taught the inhabitants how to grow vines for wine-making. As we've seen, Columbanus preferred beer, and there had probably been vines here from at least the Roman period. The reality is that this area was owned by the monastery long after Columbanus had died, so the town got its name by association with the monastery, not directly with its founder. But if the saint were to visit the town now, he'd be able to get a nice cold glass of home. On the deserted outskirts of town I saw a black sign for the Brazen Head – Irish Pub. The original Brazen Head is reputedly the oldest pub in Dublin, and its low-beamed premises sit beside the Liffey about half a mile from my house. I'd studiously avoided British and Irish pubs on my travels, but if it hadn't been closed I would have walked up to the bar in the Brazen Head in San Colombano al Lambro and drunk a pint of the black stuff to the angry saint I was following.

I found another bar that was almost as empty as the sandwich they served me, then saddled up once more. On the way into Piacenza I was fighting with trucks again on a long bridge over the Po river. I put my head down and didn't stop pedaling until I was on the other side of a roundabout on a quiet street. Margaret Stokes had come through in 1889 on her way to Bobbio, and commented: 'No tourist thinks of stopping here, so there is a delightful absence of the English element.' It's the same today, and my guidebook didn't cover Piacenza, so I was on my own in trying to find a hotel. I followed my nose to a narrow pedestrianised shopping street, and out into a large square. Warm red brick was everywhere, and in the centre a fort-like building with battlements on top and a row of white marble arches at ground level. It looked like a cross between a cathedral and a castle. This was the *broleto*, the late medieval merchants' building that marked the secular heart of the city.

But still no hotels. Down another shopping street and across an ancient canal. I was heading away from the centre. I vowed to stay in the next hotel I found, regardless of price or appearance. I should have eaten more for breakfast and lunch, and was now feeling weak and empty. Eventually, after forty-five dry-throated minutes I came upon the smart-looking Hotel Nazionale. Its three stars gleamed on the brass nameplate, and I tried to look nonchalant as I walked across the large, thickly carpeted foyer to the reception desk. The trim, grey-haired man behind the desk pulled the cuffs of his pristine white shirt down below his crisp blue jacket sleeves and smiled. A broad friendly smile. The smile of a fellow cyclist?

'*Buona sera*, sir. You come far today?' he said, somehow divining that I spoke English.

'A hundred and ten kilometres. From near Vimercate,' I said.

'Very good. I ride myself, and like the cycling very much. You look for a room? For one night, yes? I have a nice one for you.'

And he did – a smart room, breakfast and space for the bike in the underground car park for a third less than the shrugging schemer in Como had charged. Tomorrow I'd be in Bobbio, *deo volente*.

It took me ages to find a restaurant that evening, and as I wandered through the centre of town, I was worried about the next day. I just had to do what I'd been doing since leaving Dublin – get up and ride the bike – but I felt vulnerable, as if to do this big thing was to poke my head above the parapet. I'd be safer if I was still at home watching *Changing Rooms*. Something was bound to happen tomorrow, or I'd get to Bobbio and it would be a huge let-down. You can't ride from Ireland to Italy without even having a puncture. Can you?

That morning everything seemed to matter more: what I wore, what gear the bike was in, the posters on the billboards at the edge of town. To the drivers that sped past me on the flat road to Rivergaro I was just a guy on a bike, and this was just an ordinary Saturday. But my stomach was tight as I spun in an easy gear, and when the signs started giving a countdown of the distance to Bobbio at every kilometre, I couldn't quite believe I was really going to be there in a couple of hours.

After Rivergaro the curves of the green Apennines appeared ahead of me, but the road tracked the wide gravelly river, over and back across bridges and through a couple of dark tunnels. I kept telling myself to hold it together, to keep the cranks turning, not to take anything for granted, and then the road rounded a corner as the hills closed in a little and a town stretched out before me, nestling in the valley with its pale bell-towers reaching upwards. The town founded by Columbanus, and his last resting-place. I was all but there. Ahead of me I spotted a bright yellow sign beside the road – '*Benvenuti – Bienvenu* – Welcome – *Willkommen – BOBBIO, CITTÀ D'ARTE*'. I stopped for my final signpost photo, punching the air and grinning madly. I'd hardly got back on the bike when the curve unwound and I saw a full-size statue of a robed man with one hand on a crozier, the other upraised in blessing. A bird was sitting on his shoulder, and a crucifix hung round his neck. I dumped the bike on the verge and walked over to Columbanus. He was waiting for me, facing away from town with a calm expression on his bearded face. He was very different from the figure that burns with holy rage outside the church in Luxeuil. The Irishman seemed to have found a home in the hills of Italy.

Then to the town's main square, buzzing with Saturday business. All bustle and shoes and mops and mushrooms on the market stalls, like they'd thrown a party for my arrival. There was a hotel right there – and of course they'd room, and a garage for the bike – and before I knew it I was sitting on my bed with my head in my hands half laughing, half crying. Bangor to Bobbio. For six months, since the idea had launched itself at me in the Olympia Theatre, I had planned and read and ridden. And I was at the object of my quest or pilgrimage or adventure or whatever the hell I'd been doing. And I'd done it – ridden my bike across France and Switzerland to Italy, crossed the Alps and stopped in on Germany,

Liechtenstein and Austria. None of the terrible things I'd imagined had come to pass. It was as if Columbanus had been looking after me. And the first thing I had to do was pay him a visit.

23

An Irish–Italian Town

When Columbanus arrived in this valley, there had been a ruined church beside the river, and little else. He was an old man, but he did some of the hard work required to build a home for himself and his followers. Jonas tells of younger monks struggling with heavy oak beams while their abbot bent down and picked them up as if they were toothpicks. Soon there was shelter, and the church had been restored. It was a good place to be, reminiscent of the first monastery at Annegray in flat land surrounded by wooded hills. Under the terms of the grant from King Agilulf, the monks were independent of any local secular or religious control – at last Columbanus would be left alone.

The present Basilica San Colombano lies behind the site occupied by the monastery at the end of a rectangular piazza. A simple fifteenth-century construction of rough brown-red brick, it has a colonnaded entrance that leads into a long, whitewashed nave. As I walked in, a woman was washing the floor near the altar, but otherwise the church was empty. Both side aisles had flights of steps that led down into the crypt. As I put my foot on the first step, the organ broke the silence high above me, perfectly on cue – as if this were the movie version of the trip. The soundtrack swelled as I entered the large, vaulted space lit by candles and the light from three small stained-glass windows at the end of the room. In the centre there was a white marble sarcophagus with an ornate iron railing around it and on top a carving of a man lying full-length in repose. His eyes were closed below his bishop's mitre. He had a strong nose, and a long, bearded face. On one side of the tomb, beside a carving of an Irish harp, was the simple Latin inscription: '*Heic quiescat in pace Christi, S. Columbanus, Abbas.*' Here lies St Columbanus, Abbot, in the peace of Christ.

It's a beautiful place to enjoy your final rest. Kneeling down in front of Columbanus, I started to talk to him. 'I've come from Ireland to see you. I was in Bangor, and the sun was shining and you could see down the hill to the harbour. Do you remember? And then I got the boat to Brittany. I saw the beach where you landed, with the rocks out in the bay. There's a monument to you there, and your statue in the village that's named for you.

'I saw the river in Nantes where you wrote that sad letter back to the monks in Luxeuil when they were putting you on the boat to go home. And I travelled down the Loire like you did. I prayed at St Martin's tomb in Tours, where you did your vigil.

'Remember the fort in Avallon, and the Roman arch on the way into Autun? And the bend in the river at Besançon where the crag towers over the town?

'You're still remembered in Luxeuil, you know. There are statues and pictures of you in the town, and people still visit your sanctuary near Annegray, and put flowers at the mouth of the cave. I went along the Rhine and down into the lake where Gall threw the idols into the water. And over the mountains to Bregenz. There are streets with your name, and a town has sprung up where Gall went up into the hills.

'I travelled the road over the high mountains and down to that lovely lake. Queen Theodelinda is remembered too. Hundreds of Irish people followed you, you know? Your monasteries flourished for centuries.

'And now I'm here. I'm here because of you. Thanks for looking after me on the trip. I'll be around for a few days – I'll come back and see you.'

I rooted around in my wallet. There, amid the stray currency from France, Switzerland, Austria and Italy, I found a crumpled five-pound note I'd carried with me from Ireland. I wanted to leave Columbanus something from home, and this was all I could think of. I folded the note and slipped it into the collection box.

It was strange to be talking to a dead saint in a language he'd never heard, but no more so than following his route on a bike through eight countries. Knowing Columbanus, he would have been unmoved by my efforts. I'd been too lazy and much too godless to impress him. I admired his rigour, and was jealous of his conviction, but I was no longer so anxious to be like him. I'd hoped the trip would change me, or provide me with some direction. But now I was nearly done, and the only bit of me that had really changed was my legs. I still worried, and still had no idea what I was going to do next, but I didn't mind so much any more. I'd go back to Dublin, start writing this up as a book, and see what happened.

That night I feasted like a farmer in a restaurant across the square from the hotel. As in the place on my first night beside the Loire, I just sat down and they brought me what they'd been cooking until I couldn't eat any more. I hoovered up pasta with beans, slabs of lamb and thick greasy discs of salami, brown and white pickled onions, artichoke hearts and overcooked veggies. The television was on in the corner, and if I didn't fancy a particular dish, I just passed on it and waited for the next steaming platter to arrive from the kitchen.

At the table next to me a group of young lads were eating even more seriously than I was. Two were twins, and they looked so Irish I was convinced they were from Ballahadreen not Bobbio. They had fair skin, long jaws and foreheads, small eyes and a sprinkling of freckles. There was almost no conversation interrupting the ingestion of large quantities of heavy food, and the scene wouldn't have been out of place at a Tipperary farmer's table, but it was hard to guess the twins' nationality. Their friends looked more traditionally Italian, but it was only when one of the brothers asked the waitress for more bread that I knew they were all locals.

But I'm sure there was some Celtic blood in those veins. No doubt a young Irish monk had arrived at the monastery a few years after Columbanus had died. Overcome by the fragrant Italian air and the beautiful Apennine scenery, he had fallen for a sultry young temptress from the village and renounced his vows to marry her and raise goats and children. The two lads sitting across from me were his direct descendants.

That story might be a little far-fetched, but the citizens of Bobbio certainly know all about their Irish connections. Next morning I visited the tourist office, which was in a fetching green Portakabin that I could see from my hotel window. Sabina had just come back from Navan in County

Meath, the agricultural town whose most famous son is James Bond actor Pierce Brosnan. Plans are afoot to twin Navan with Bobbio. It's not hard to see who gets the better end of that deal: you're a local councillor in Meath, and you get to come to a beautiful historic town between Milan and Bologna for a jolly. Or you're a Bobbio councillor who goes to Navan and gets taken on a tour of the livestock mart.

But Sabina wasn't complaining. She'd enjoyed it in Ireland and was telling me where the local kids go on their school trips. 'Every year we go to Luxeuil or St Gallen and Bregenz, so all the children know the stories. Some years we would like to go somewhere else, but everyone who grew up in the town has been to see the other monasteries.'

'You're kidding. So Columbanus is still important to people here?'

She laughed. 'Of course. He founded the town. Until recently boys here had the name Colombano. But not any more so much.'

So my nephew Columbanus in south London shares his Irish-Latin name with generations of men from northern Italy.

Sabina wouldn't let me leave without armfuls of leaflets and maps, and she told me how to get to one of the caves associated with Columbanus. Local legend had it that he died at the grotto, which is dedicated to St Michael. She also made me promise I'd visit the museum that had recently been opened in part of the restored monastery.

When Margaret Stokes had visited, she'd had a tour of what remained of it, and found the refectory being used as a macaroni factory. In the crypt of the basilica, the recumbent statue of the saint had been standing up against the wall.

Now, of course, the crypt is in excellent shape, and the monastery has had a makeover too. Four or five inter-connected rooms house a selection of monastic artefacts, from the eighth-century carved slab that topped Abbot Cummian's sepulchre to the sixteenth-century reliquary for the bust of St Columbanus.

There was no escaping the Irish element in many of the exhibits. The ornate carvings on the back of Cummian's stone are pure Celtic knotwork, with the same intricate patterns I'd seen in the books at St Gallen. The inscription on the front records how 'Scotia [Ireland] sent him here to the boundaries of Italy in his old age … He lived in such happiness we may believe him now to be blessed. Merciful, prudent, pious to the brethren, peaceful with all men.' And many of the brethren he led had made the same journey from Ireland. For centuries after the death of Columbanus, Irish monks travelled to Bobbio, where the scriptorium became famous for the quality of the books it produced. As at St Gallen, they offered Continental versions of a distinctly Irish style. The locals seemed proud of their Celtic roots. As well they should: Bobbio was an Irish town three hundred years before Dublin was founded by the Vikings.

I walked back along the main street past the wine merchant, greengrocer and mushroom shop (mushrooms are big in Bobbio – Sabina told me that they were holding a festival the following Sunday, which included a church service to give thanks for the blessed fungi), down the hill to the river, and over the new road that diverts the traffic for Genoa away from the centre. An ancient Roman bridge stretched across the broad banks of the river Trebbia, about as wide as a horse-drawn cart. I walked to the middle and sat on the side, looking back at the red-tiled roofs of the town, and the steep hills behind. The leaves on some of the trees were beginning to turn – conkers had been falling off the horse-chestnut trees outside my window during the night and crashing on to the glass conservatory below.

The summer was over, and I'd spent all morning thinking about the connections between this place and Ireland. I got my bearings and looked away to the north-west over the hills. It was the first time in the whole journey that I'd stopped to work out which way was home.

But there was still Columbanus's cave to visit. Sabina had said it was a little way beyond Coli, a small village over to the west of Bobbio. One of my new maps showed a footpath that climbed up from the other side of the bridge. Although the grey clouds suggested rain, it was time for a Sunday stroll, and I was soon into thick woods across the river. What had been a clear red dotted line on the map turned out to be little more than wishful thinking on the ground. At the first fork in the path, still within earshot of the river, there were no signs to help me and I ended up wandering around someone's vineyard. Back to the fork, and the path became a bent-double uphill fight through vicious briars. My cycling shoes weren't designed for the combination of mud and wet rock, and the metal cleats skittered as I slipped and slid. At intervals painted wooden pointers were nailed to trees, but they were more a joke than a guide.

After nearly an hour of scrabbling, the path delivered me to a road – you mean I could have walked up the road? Below, Bobbio didn't seem very far away for all my effort. Ahead, the road passed between a small house and a barn, and as I approached a huge dog started barking wildly inside the barn and throwing itself against the walls. It could smell a cyclist even when I wasn't on my bike.

It was no use. I was at least another two hours from Coli, where I'd still have to find the cave, and it had started to rain. I carefully retraced my steps, tiptoeing past the angry dog (he was still bouncing off the walls) and fearing for my knees and ankles down the steep paths to the river.

I needed coffee. Back in Bobbio, the streets were empty – everyone was home having their Sunday lunch – but one café was open, and its outdoor tables were covered with a white canopy. An older couple and a young woman occupied one table, and as I sat down near them, I heard the unmistakable sound of Irish accents. Terry and Mary were from Clonmel, and they were over visiting their Italian friend Paola. They'd been in Rome, and were now travelling north to Paola's home in Milan. Terry was ragging Paola for saying 'rock time' instead of 'Stone Age'. 'We've been to Italy quite a lot, and I knew that if we ever got the chance I'd like to come here to see St Columbanus,' said Terry.

'Why were you interested?'

'I don't know, really. He's an important Irishman, and he's not very well remembered at home.'

Of course there were Irish people for me to meet in Bobbio. The whole day had been full of remembrances of the country. My book on pilgrimages told me that there were three stages to be undertaken: separation, journey and reintegration. The pilgrim – even an accidental one – has to go home, and talking with Terry and Mary felt like the first step towards reintegration.

★

Another day, another attempt on the cave. This time I was going by bike, and I was looking forward to a final climb, especially with the panniers left in their customary exploded state in the hotel room. There was a hazy sun, and the incline started as soon as I'd turned off the main road. It was a great climb, with switchbacks cutting through the woods and a view down to the river far below. I was dancing up the slope, getting much more response from the lightened bike as I kicked out of the saddle. Soon my arm warmers were round my wrists, and the road straightened as it led to the village. I was a sad case, smiling broadly as my legs began to ache.

It appears that it also took Margaret Stokes two attempts to reach the cave during her visit. In a letter home she describes the first effort dismissively: 'We had a stupid guide who did not know the way.' I know how that feels. But she had much better luck when she tried again, and was taken by the scenery: 'I wish you could have seen the fine gorges, the cliffs, the oak and chestnut forests, the rocky beds of the torrents through which our brave old saint had to scramble to reach this last resting-place, and you would have felt that there was something wonderful about it all.'

She was right. I left the bike in the main piazza in Coli and continued on foot down a path that was rough but easy to follow as it dropped to a busy stream. Over the stone bridge it climbed steeply into the trees, and at intervals bright blue crosses were painted on rocks beside the path. Here Margaret had met a second guide, who half carried her up the steeper parts. It must have been quite an endeavour, especially as she brought her heavy tripod camera with her – in her lodgings back in Bobbio, she'd taken an extra room for use as a dark-room.

After half an hour of walking, the way forked and a hand-painted sign pointed the way to 'San Michele'. I picked my way along a narrow path next to a steep drop with the sound of the stream below very loud amid the silence. The path stopped beneath a cliff-face, on a lip no wider than eight feet. A tumble of stones showed where a tiny building must have been. Fixed to the rough cliff wall at head-height was a metal cross. Each arm was of equal length, with curved scrollwork at the ends. Overlying the flat metal was a simple interlaced design of three-stranded wire. It stood proud from the rock face, and as the dappled sunlight came through the trees, the stone shone white behind it and the cross seemed to float in the air. It was a powerful and beautiful symbol, and a very Irish thing to find deep in an Italian forest.

I sat on one of the rocks for a while. This was the furthest point from home I was going to reach. With the kilometres from Bobbio to Coli, and the miles I'd done up to Bangor, the full distance I'd ridden came to a nice round two thousand miles.

Columbanus had had less than two years to enjoy his Italian home. He was slowly weakening, and in November 615 he became ill. His thoughts turned to Gall, back over the Alps. He had heard that his old friend had established a community, and he ordered his pastoral staff to be sent northwards to Gall, as a sign of friendship after their dispute. It was perhaps the closest Columbanus ever came to an apology. That same night, Gall had a vision in which he saw that his old friend had died. He sent a deacon to Bobbio to find out if this was true. It was. The deacon returned to

Switzerland with Columbanus's staff, and Gall undertook to say continual masses and prayers to the memory of the saint.

Gall had outlived his master, and his master's enemies in France. Although Theuderic and Brunhilda had defeated Theudebert, their victory was short-lived. Theuderic died of dysentery soon after, and King Chlotar, who had welcomed Columbanus when he avoided exile in Nantes, defeated Brunhilda's forces and united the Frankish kingdoms. Brunhilda suffered a particularly unpleasant fate. Having been paraded on a camel, she was torn apart by wild horses. Columbanus would no doubt have considered this harsh but fair, like a crunching tackle on someone who wronged you last season.

The monasteries that Columbanus had founded lived on long after him, some for a thousand years and more. Within a century of his death, over a hundred sister foundations had sprung up, led by his pupils and continuing many of his traditions. Over time, his harsh Rule was replaced with the more humane approach of the Benedictines, but Irishmen still crossed the Continent to study and work in his houses. And one element of Columbanus's Irish teachings was to have a dramatic influence. In the Church of the sixth and seventh centuries in France and Italy, penance was regarded as a public, one-time-only deal. Those looking to clear their spiritual debts had to confess their sins publicly and turn their backs on their former lives, becoming permanent penitents.

The Irish approach, as practised by Columbanus, was for regular private confession. Monks confessed to their close companions, and once they had carried out the required penance, they were absolved of their sins. This custom

became widely practised across the Continent, and formed
the basis of the later Catholic Church's system of confession.

Monday evening, and everywhere was closed. The streets
were deserted again, as if the residents were only allowed out
at set times of day. The restaurant in the hotel was closed,
and so was the one with the huge farming feasts. *And* the one
I'd eaten in the previous night. Then I'd walked in and said,
'*Per uno, per favore,*' which seemed pretty self-explanatory.
But the waiter had taken me outside, in through a side door
and along a dark corridor, switching on the lights as we
went. The restaurant had been almost empty, so I was
confused. Perhaps a coach party was expected, or they had
a different dining room for foreigners. I thought of stopping
the guy, but I wanted to see where he led me. In the end he
threw open the door of a hotel room and ushered me in.

'*Va bene?*' he asked.

I started laughing, trying to work out the Italian for 'I only
wanted something to eat, and if this is your way of getting me
to pay the bill, you can forget it, pal,' but instead I told him that
I only wanted some food. The young man laughed and apologised, and we returned rather sheepishly to the restaurant.

But now I might be reduced to more bedroom adventures
to get a meal. I half remembered reading about another
restaurant on the other side of town, but as I walked and
walked, it looked like I'd finally need those two emergency
energy bars at the bottom of my panniers. At last I came
upon a small restaurant and hotel with large windows out on
to the street. A couple was dining inside. I went in gratefully.
The couple were from France, and the proprietor was
speaking French to them, outlining what was on offer, which

I reckoned was pretty much whatever his family was having for dinner that night.

The food was good, but no one else joined the party, and my fellow diners headed off upstairs a little before I finished. As I was leaving, I complimented the owner on his good French, and we fell to talking. I told him about my trip, and he told me that he was from Bobbio, but had lived in Turin for a long time. He'd returned a few years ago, and liked the scenery and the quiet pace of life. I was talking in French to an Italian about an Irishman – it felt like the whole event had been set up for me to mark my last night in Bobbio. He poured me a liqueur on the house, and I taught him to say, '*Sláinte*,' as we drank to St Columbanus.

24

Lap of Honour

Before I left Bobbio, I went to say goodbye to Columbanus and bought a credit-card-sized remembrance from the Icomatic machine upstairs from the crypt. The machine looks like a cigarette-vending box, with coin slot and drawer for collecting your choice of icon. Columbanus's card has a picture of him on one side, and a prayer on the other. I pondered the life of an Icomatic salesman. Do they sit in smoke-filled meeting rooms discussing their sales targets for the next year?

'What do you mean St Columbanus isn't selling? He's a national hero, no, an international hero. You've got adventure, miracles, outdoor sports – he's a goldmine.'

'But you know what kids today are like. It's all crystals and camomile tea. Columbanus is too hardcore for them. They're going for St Francis of Assisi and the cute little animals.'

The hardcore saint's statue watched me as I rode out of town, heading back towards Primrose's near Milan. Now I was on holiday.

First stop was the Hotel Nazionale in Piacenza again, and I still couldn't find where they'd hidden all the restaurants in that town. I contented myself with an exploration of the

260

channels on my television. It was a choice between *Sabrina the Teenage Witch* in German or *Robot Wars* in Italian. Dubbing was everywhere, and there seemed to be a requirement in the homegrown programming for scantily clad women, regardless of the subject matter.

Much of Italian TV looks like it's still 1978, and the country is entranced by the debatable delights of the variety show – you can't move for big performance numbers, sequined top hats and three costume changes for the unctuous host.

The only alternative was the extensive sports coverage, where the highlight was computer-modelled fouls and goal-mouth incidents. As well as showing a suspicious dive from as many camera angles as possible, programmers then map it in 3-D and render it in a full-screen version that can be zoomed, frozen and spun *ad infinitum*. Of course, this flashy stuff assumes you have football matches to show in the first place. But not having the rights to Champions League matches didn't stop RAI offering a three-hour footie-fest on evenings when there were games. A panel of experts watched the matches on monitors in front of them. When something happened in one of the games, someone piped up, and described the event that we couldn't see. One of the low-rent cable channels I stumbled across offered a cheaper solution: just have one man at a desk, giving live commentary on the game he's watching. It's televised radio commentary – ninety minutes of staring at the top of a bloke's head.

One feature I did like was the way the Italian weather forecast is read by an air-force officer in full uniform. This adds a certain gravitas to the description of a ridge of low pressure sweeping northwards from the Mediterranean –

lives (or at least hairstyles) are at stake if there's drizzle in Milan.

The next destination on my lap of honour was Cremona, a city of such grace that I was instantly besotted. It has given the world Monteverdi, Stradivarius violins and nougat, but kept the best stuff for itself. The central piazza contains a white marble cathedral, a tall red-brick campanile, a hexagonal baptistery and a colonnaded *broleto*. By night, a dark blue velvet sky descended and the buildings were lit like film stars. I sat outside a café in the piazza with a glass of champagne – why the hell not? The air was soft and mild and there was a chatter of conversation from the denim-clad teenagers sitting on the steps in front of the cathedral. At around nine forty-five, two elderly men arrived, sat down beneath the bell-tower and laid out their chess set. The whole scene was so beautiful it would break your heart.

Pavia came to prominence in the millennium before last, and it's been taking it easy for the last eleven hundred years. After a seventy-five-kilometre ride from Cremona escorted by rain and big trucks, I was grateful for the peace and quiet of the centre of town with its ancient university and bizarrely unfinished cathedral. Its rough brick exterior was supposed to be covered in multi-coloured marble at some point in the sixteenth century, but it never happened so, as the guidebook rather cruelly said, it looks like it was finished in corrugated cardboard.

There was a lot to see, including some churches that were much earlier (and much more complete) than the cathedral, but I wasn't getting help from the tourist office.

'Is there an Internet café in town?' I asked politely.

'Yes, near the castle,' replied the young customer-focused local-government officer.

'Great.'

'Do you have a map?'

'No, that would be really helpful ...'

'Oh, well. It's near the castle, anyway. Goodbye.'

Without her help, I found my way to the tomb of the famous thinker Boethius, who is currently contemplating the consolation of philosophy from inside a very small box. Opting instead for the consolation of buying expensive sportswear, I acquired a trick pair of trainers when I decided that eight weeks wearing the same shoes was a crime in such a well-dressed country. Even before the purchase I had been stopped for directions by a young Italian lad, which was a great boost to my ego. Primrose had said she could see how I'd be taken for Swiss (which had hurt), and she could just about imagine me passing myself off as French, but had sworn that no one would ever mistake me for an Italian.

Riding through Italian towns is hard. The roads are narrow and the traffic wayward, but the biggest problem is the terrible signs. It's guesswork as to which road leading out from the centre will take you where you want to go, so after I'd seen Melzo from several different angles, I finally made it to Gorgonzola. There I rode round and round for a while without even the promise of any cheese to keep me amused. I was passing the railway station again when a motorbike came up behind me at speed. I tucked in close to the kerb, but as I crossed a junction the motorbike passed, then cut violently across me to turn right. As it was happening, I was sure he'd hit me. And then the motorbike was screaming off down the road, the moment was already in the past and I was still cycling along. The event was so binary that I couldn't quite take it in – either he crashed into me and everything was bad, or he missed me and everything was good, as if it had never happened. The world had shivered for an instant. All the way from Dublin, I'd had scarcely any near misses on the bike, even when riding through steep tunnels on the side of mountains in the dark. And now this happened, in the last twenty kilometres of the trip.

I was shaken, and all I wanted to do was get off the bike. I started singing to take my mind off my own mortality, and spun out the last half an hour. I rolled up gratefully at Primrose's house in the mid-afternoon. There was no reception committee or crowds or balloons, nothing to mark the end of my ride across Europe. I just got off the bike, leant it against the wall outside the garage, and started pulling the panniers off the rack. I tugged at the handle on one and half of it came off in my hand. My bombproof, waterproof, everything-proof Ortliebs had been the most dependable bit of kit I'd ever owned. Even they were feeling the strain. It was definitely time to stop.

25

Sad Departures

It's seven ten a.m. and I'm sitting in Linate airport with the bike beside me. It's still dark outside and the only passengers around are businessmen in suits getting the first planes to somewhere.

Primrose has dropped me here, and as we sped along the foggy motorway I was very glad I wasn't riding the bike to the airport. I'm early, as she had an appointment she had to get back for, but that's fine. The Aer Lingus check-in desk isn't open yet, and I can't leave the bike unattended while I find some breakfast, so I crack open the packet of lemon biscuits I'd been planning to take home.

There have been better mornings to be flying with a large metal object – last night American and British forces started attacking Afghanistan, so security is going to be intense. But I've called ahead to check about bringing the bike and was told that there's no problem, so I can't do any more.

It's now ten forty-five and I've got a lot of problems. First, I can't collect my ticket (the one that I'd booked and paid for). The people at the check-in desk can see I have a reservation, and can even allocate a seat for me, but due to some incompatibility between their systems, they can't print out the ticket for me to hand it straight back to them. I was assured there'd be no problem collecting my ticket at the airport. I was misinformed. Now the only way I'm getting on the flight is if I buy another ticket.

I buy another ticket. I return to the check-in desk wheeling my bike, and the woman at the desk says, 'Where's the box for your bike?'

'I was told I didn't need one, that you had all the packaging here.'

'Oh, no. You were misinformed.'

'Tell me about it.'

They'll take the bike, but it will be at my own risk. The bike is surely fucked. After getting me all the way here.

But all of this is moot now, because there's an announcement that due to 'operational reasons', the airport is closed. That's *chiuso*. No flights are getting in or out and they're going to try to find a coach to take us to Malpensa – the other Milan airport (doesn't that mean 'ill thought-out' or 'bad idea' in Italian?). No one's saying for sure what's happened, but one of the Irish guys here waiting for the flight heard that an SAS plane (I think that's Scandinavian Air Services, not the British special forces, but today you can't be sure) had skidded on take-off and was stuck on the runway or something. So it's hurry up and wait at the moment.

Still waiting. There are a lot of police around here now, and a pack of journalists just arrived, the TV folks with their cameras in those blue PortaBrace covers that show they're not messing around. Something serious has happened.

There's an airportful of people being moved. I think we're

just as likely to end up in Turin or Genoa as Malpensa, and God knows if there'll be a plane to meet us. I'm really hungry now.

Just waiting near the British Airways desk and a businessman is arguing with the Italian BA woman. 'You don't understand,' he says. 'I have to get to Heathrow to make the connection to New York.'

'I'm sorry, sir, but the airport is closed. We're doing everything we can to get people to their destinations as quickly as possible.'

'But that's just not good enough. When will I be in London?'

'I can't tell you that because I'm afraid I don't know. Everyone's moving to Malpensa.'

'There must be something you can do. I've been flying with BA for twenty years. You have to get me on a flight to Heathrow now.'

'Sir, the airport's closed. Everyone is in the same situation. If you could just be patient.'

'I will not be patient. This is unbelievable!'

Suddenly the woman looks tired. She pauses, then says steadily, 'There are people dead outside. You'll just have to wait.'

I head off to find a bathroom. There are no windows in the terminal building (an unfortunate term, it now strikes me), so I can't see what might be happening outside, but the air-conditioning system is pumping acrid air into the gents.

The coaches arrive to take us to Malpensa, and I wrestle the bike and panniers down the crowded stairs and out to the kerb. With the handlebars turned round for stowing it's difficult to steer and on one tricky corner the front wheel slides out, tipping the bike so the chain-ring takes a bite out of my shin. The worst cycling injury I've sustained and I wasn't even riding the bike.

It's cumbersome as hell, but there are no arguments – the bike is going with me, so I slide it into the belly of the coach and climb aboard. The atmosphere is muted – word has got round about the plane crash and although there are no details yet it sounds serious. Everyone's being polite, and people are talking in hushed tones. I sit next to this guy Seán, who's from Limerick and had been in Italy visiting his girlfriend.

As the coach edges out of the airport we see emergency vehicles and TV vans parked by a gate. In the distance the white and blue tail section of a plane is tilted at an odd angle, very close to the walls of a low building. There's smoke still rising lazily from the scene.

We learnt later that an SAS jet had crashed on take-off into a small plane on the runway, then careered into the baggage-handling building. The plane exploded and the roof of the building collapsed on top of it. Over a hundred people had been killed.

We reach Malpensa and things happen smoothly. The incoming flight from Dublin had been diverted here when Linate closed, so a plane is waiting to take us home. We check in again, and I wheel my bike over to the oversized-baggage area. The only protection the bike has is a forlorn luggage tag looped around the crossbar. I should have tried to find some plastic sheeting or something, but there's no time, and I don't care any more. I say goodbye to my good honest bicycle and hand it to the baggage-handler. 'There are people dead outside' – my bike doesn't matter very much.

Out at the gate, people are sharing food and drink. Seán appears with a *panino* and tears off half for me. I root around and find a slab of chocolate I was going to take home.

We get on to another bus to take us out to the plane. Next to me, an Italian woman in her mid-thirties is struggling to make a phone call on a heavy old mobile. In the end, she turns to me. 'Please, can you talk to my boyfriend and tell him I think I miss my plane to Shannon? My English is not good.'

'Sure. What's your name?'

'Bruna. My boyfriend, he meets me in Shannon.'

'I just hit Send? … Hi, you don't know me but I'm one of Bruna's fellow travellers on the flight from Milan. We've been delayed and Bruna might not make her connection from Dublin. We're just leaving Milan now.'

'Er … right. Tell her to call me when she gets to Dublin and let me know if she's on the Shannon flight.'

It turns out Seán's car is in Dublin, and he's driving down to Limerick. He offers to give Bruna a lift if she misses her connection. This wouldn't happen on an ordinary day.

I say goodbye to Seán and Bruna in the baggage hall in Dublin airport. I've got my panniers, but I'm waiting at the oversized-luggage carousel for what's left of the bike. After fifteen minutes, there's no sign of it so I walk back to the carousel for the ordinary luggage from the flight. There, leaning up against a pillar, is the Dawes, in perfect shape. It looks like it had been teleported from Malpensa.

Epilogue

I've been back in Dublin for a while now, and have settled into a familiar rhythm. Despite my best efforts to avoid working in an office again, my savings ran out and now I'm riding my long-suffering touring bike to work down the East Wall Road (and still haven't had any punctures).

Sometimes I wonder if I really did ride my bike two thousand miles across Europe in pursuit of a sixth-century monk. It just seems so bizarre; you'd have to be mad to do something like that, wouldn't you? But then I'll be pulling out my wallet in my local, and I'll see the St Columbanus Icomatic card I bought in Bobbio, and I remember – this unlikely and potentially life-threatening endeavour was perhaps the best thing I've ever done. For a brief while I stepped outside ordinary expectations, and lived on the road as a traveller, a pilgrim, a guest of the world.

And if I walk around town apparently unaffected by those months, you shouldn't get the wrong idea. I wasn't changed in a huge way, and Columbanus is perhaps too extreme a figure to model yourself on, but I returned from the trip happier about not having any answers. I started work on this book, and a year after the trip, I was back in Italy, where I met someone through a mutual friend. Someone who, unbelievably, thinks both Celtic saints and bicycles are sexy. Using a seduction technique based on cups of tea and embarrassment, I won her over, and we've since got married. The reception was held in Glendalough, next to the beautiful monastic site founded by Columbanus's colleague St Kevin. Columbanus himself couldn't make it, but as we dashed out into the rainy ruins for some photographs, I spared a thought for him lying in his tomb in far-away Bobbio. He'd been a great travelling companion.

Acknowledgements

I am very grateful to the many people who helped me turn a stray idea into this book. Garrett Fagan, Paul Clerkin and Mick Cunningham provided good-natured encouragement and support throughout the long process. Dave Walsh and Miles Bly generously showed me how real cyclists do things, while my sister Uma Dinsmore-Tuli was so enthusiastic as to name her second son for the irascible saint I followed. At Hodder Headline Ireland, Ciara Considine's insights and suggestions acted as a form of psychiatry for me, and greatly improved my work. And finally, Marci Riskin ensured the book has a happy ending – I am in her debt for that, as for so much else. Of course, responsibility for any mistakes that remain rests with me.